"Dusty, Here!"

Understanding a Dog's Point of View

By
Duff Lueder
and
Bettie LaDuke

authorHOUSE™

1663 LIBERTY DRIVE, SUITE 200
BLOOMINGTON, INDIANA 47403
(800) 839-8640
WWW.AUTHORHOUSE.COM

First published by AuthorHouse 09/08/04

ISBN: 1-4184-6863-0 (sc)

Printed in the United States of America
Bloomington, Indiana

This book is printed on acid-free paper.

Illustrations by Candace Brown
Portraits by Duff Lueder
Contributing photographers: Gene Baruch, Bonnie Meyers, and Neil Tepper

"Helping Dogs with People Problems"

Duff Lueder grew up without ever having a dog of his own. He did, however, learn about dogs between the ages of 12 and 14 by spending two weeks every summer with his aunt and uncle on their farm, in the constant company of their Collie (with whom he played), whose job was to gather the cows at milking time.

The bond and relationship which developed eventually culminated one day when the Collie knocked Duff down into a ditch in an obvious effort to keep him from entering into the path of an oncoming car that Duff didn't see when attempting to cross the road.

This demonstration of devotion of one friend for another, particularly when manifested between one species and another, has always been something Duff is very grateful for and a very cherished memory. It wasn't until later in life and during his law enforcement career that the opportunity to understand, appreciate, and re-establish that bond between dog and human manifested itself, when he became a certified K-9 handler of Man Tracking and Article Search dogs, Narcotic Detection dogs, Explosives Detection dogs, and Image (or Public Relations) dogs. The training resulted in the understanding of how dogs learn, think, and perceive their surroundings, as well as how to learn to communicate with them in ways they can properly relate to, based on their view and understanding of the world. These dogs were overt, dominant personalities that were self motivated and loved their work. Duff learned very quickly from his American and German trainers that his dogs didn't do things just because they loved him and he was human (although humans would like to think this is the case), but rather because it felt good and worked for the dog first, and that the bond with the human came second and when the combination came together, it was wonderful! He learned that training your dog was not about egos, as dogs don't have concerns in that area. It was not about dominating the dog into submission, using collars and leashes as tools of discipline (as has so widely been practiced over the last 70 years of organized training); and it was not about having a master/slave relationship, with you being the "boss" and the dog having to abide by your will like some robot.

As a result of this training and a greater understanding of dog/human teamwork, Duff opened his own private dog training facility for the public in 1981. He started additional education for the public through local television programs, public speaking events, and college lectures, where he combined drug education with the K-9 program, showing how the dog's sense of smell and special abilities can save human lives. Today Duff, along with his wife Jane, are the co-founders and Master Trainers of KNINEPAL Dog Training. They exclusively make house calls nationwide as well as train over the internet, giving one-on-one, customized instruction, from puppy to adult dog behavioral and training problems. The KNINEPAL PROCESS teaches the human leaders how to train their own dogs based on their abilities, the abilities of the dog, and the environmental conditions in which they live.

Duff has incorporated what he learned in early training, as well as what he has learned from the dogs themselves over the years, into a training process designed to bring about the bonding and respect between humans and their dogs in the way he first felt with the Collie he played with as a child. He also knows that this training process must be flexible enough to deal with the fact that no two dogs are alike anymore than any two humans are alike. It is designed to open up minds to "non-traditional" ways of understanding, communicating, and teaching dogs what it is we expect from them and what they can expect from us. He believes these relationships are to be based on respect and understanding, not domination and confrontation just because we can. We also need to understand that well-mannered and obedient dogs do not happen by accident or chance. It is the result of a commitment of their human leaders of time, patience, love, respect, and a proven and tried training process that also teaches how their dogs learn, think, and act based on their view of the world.

Duff believes that dog training is supposed to be fun, not only for the human leaders, but for the dog. Dogs love having fun and learning new things. They also have been human subordinate for an estimated 15,000 years. They WILL follow if their human leader will lead. Leadership of the pack is what dogs instinctively understand. If dogs do not see leadership from their human leader in certain aspects of day-to-day interaction, they will instinctively attempt to insert themselves into the role. When this happens, we as humans don't always like the results. The responsibility to fix this is not the dog's but ours as human leaders.

Duff teaches that the fundamental problem that occurs between humans and their dogs originates from the inability to properly communicate in a way that the dog can naturally relate to. Dogs do not speak "human", and humans do not regularly speak "dog", so the communication gap results in mixed signals and misunderstandings. Dogs do not communicate through verbiage as we do, but, rather, by watching and initiating body language and posturing. So while humans are talking their dogs' ears off with complete sentences, pulling and manipulating them around on a leash, and yelling "No" at them in an attempt to affirm our dislike for a specific behavior, they are frantically trying to figure out what our body language means at the moment. This is stressful, frustrating, and doesn't work very well!

As a by-product of the communication breakdown, dogs that do unacceptable behaviors (unless it is a health-related issue) are the result of the dog being insufficiently trained, insufficiently socialized, and/or insufficiently supervised. Weaknesses in these areas do not mean that the humans are bad dog owners. These are common communication and training issues that don't just automatically work themselves out. So this is where KNINEPAL TRAINING and LEADERSHIP programs come in to assist and guide dog owners and their dogs to success, with one-on-one instruction Learning to speak "dog" involves the proper and specific implementation of body language and hand signals in addition to one-syllable vocal tone commands that help dogs naturally understand what it is we mean.

Duff is controversial with some when he declares that there is NOT a one-size-fits-all methodology of training that fits any dog, nor is there one training book that has all the answers. Teaching and training living things requires that the process be flexible to accommodate abilities and limitations of the students. His "KNINEPAL Dog and Owner-Centered Learning" procedures are recognized humane techniques that are customized and geared to fit individual concerns, lifestyles, personalities, and abilities of the dog and human leader. Old techniques of training are not to be discarded and dismissed, but rather to be added to, refined, and designed to work as we learn more. Duff does not believe that his process is the best way, the right way, or the only way. It is simply "another" way based on education and experience.

A "Mom" Recalls...

March 3

I awoke to the sound of heavy rain. It didn't matter. Nothing would keep me from meeting my very own puppy. I had never had a puppy of my own. When I was growing up, we always had a family dog. My sisters have dogs. I love dogs. Until recently I had traveled most of the time on my job and could not have any kind of a pet. When my job changed and I was no longer required to travel, thoughts of having a dog of my own began to creep into my mind. What kind should I get?

I wanted a male dog because my family always had male dogs. I wanted an independent dog—one that wouldn't mope all day while I was at work. As a single person, no one would be home during the day. I wanted a dog that didn't shed, wouldn't grow to be heavier than 30 pounds, and wasn't plagued with disease and allergies due to over-breeding. I wanted a cute dog—"fuzzy" would be good.

After conducting a lot of research on various breeds of dogs, I decided on a Welsh Terrier. Never mind the fact that they are relatively difficult to find and that breeders interview you intensively before agreeing even to consider you as a potential "parent" to a Welsh Terrier. The breeders with whom I "interviewed," as well as the articles I read about Welsh Terriers, stressed the fact that WTs, while very special dogs, tend to be dominant dogs and require household rules to be established and enforced. A common interview question was, "Are you familiar with the terrier personality?" I was. My twin sister had had a Scottish Terrier, whom we both loved. I remembered his intelligence and strong will. No problem. I could handle that. I was put on a waiting list to receive a male Welsh Terrier. I could hardly wait. I had already chosen a name for him—Dusty Thomas. Dusty was "cute". Thomas was more "sophisticated", to reflect his European roots. Five months passed, and I still didn't have a puppy. Then I saw one advertised in the local paper. One male Welsh Terrier, 14 weeks old. I was on my way to meet him. I was sure I would love him at first sight.

I rang the doorbell. The excitement was building. I met the breeder and the breeder's dog. Then I met Dusty Thomas. Well, sorta. He was a wild puppy. Literally. He appeared out of nowhere—running as fast as he could from one room to another, chasing the breeder's dog. The breeder tackled him and handed him to me. He chewed on my hands and clawed my neck. He was warm, but not cuddly. I was dismayed. I didn't remember any of our family puppies being so aggressive. But…I immediately went into denial. After waiting this long, there was no way this puppy could be the wrong puppy for me. He was my longed-for WT. He would be fine when I got him home.

I carried Dusty Thomas to the car and put him in it. (Just in case I would decide not to keep him, I had not yet purchased a crate.) What a mistake! Driving in heavy rain, I had to wrestle with this puppy all the way home to keep him out of my lap and from bouncing up into my face. He didn't like the windshield wipers and became more and more hyper. He chewed up my hands. I stopped at the pet store to buy a crate (and toys). With Dusty in my arms (I couldn't leave him in the car), I let the salesman talk me into a crate that I knew was too large. (I had researched crates and crate training too.) We were both exhausted when we got home, and we both collapsed for a brief period of time.

When Dusty awoke from his nap, I tried to play with him. He became "wild dog" again. He raced through the house, jumped on furniture, jumped on me, knocked over the fireplace tools, tugged on the vertical blinds, and pulled clothes off of low-hanging hangers in the closet. He chomped down on my arm when I nudged him off coffee tables, and I literally had to pry his mouth away from my arm. Something was wrong with this picture. I cried, put the puppy in his crate, and went to sleep. Fortunately, Dusty cried and fussed in his crate for only 10 minutes.

March 4

I woke up and went to the other room to get Dusty. He was warm and cuddly, and the day started off well. It didn't last long. His wild antics, some of which were entertaining but most of which were not, and his destructive behavior continued. There was no stopping him. I did laugh as I realized that while I was standing at the vanity getting ready for church, there was constant tornado-like activity behind me. How my life had changed in less than 24 hours! He ran under the bed and chewed on a plastic sweater box; he chewed on the corners of books in the bookcase; he nibbled at a plant; and he chased my feet and nipped at my ankles. This continued all day long. I was too naïve and ignorant of how to manage a puppy to know that I needed to put him in his crate—frequently. My family had never crated a dog, and I thought crates were just for sleeping. I would soon learn differently.

Dusty was a little "devil"!

March 5

I went to work and told my boss and my colleagues that I had done something very stupid over the weekend—I had purchased a puppy. "You didn't just adopt an older dog?" someone asked. I described the activities of the weekend, and my boss and colleagues were very supportive. Many had suggestions, including drop-kicking the puppy across the room like a football, planting my knee in his chest, choking him with a choke collar, bopping him on his nose with a rolled-up newspaper, and, of course, returning him. The end of my 72-hour trial period with the puppy was near. I could do none of the things that were suggested. Well, except bopping him on his nose with a newspaper. I tried that. He fought back—stood up on his hind legs and waved his front legs, biting at my arm! Distraught as I was, Dusty Thomas was mine, my own WT, and some way, somehow we were going to bond with each other and be happy.

I returned home after work. I had left the pet door open so Dusty could go outside whenever he wanted to. (I had thought of everything before I made the big purchase.) I would not have been surprised to find that Dusty had escaped from my fenced-in yard. He was still there—in his room. He wagged his tail and was happy to see me. I picked him up and took him outside, giving him a quick kiss on the top of his curly head as I did so. He was cute, if nothing else. He turned his little head and licked me on the neck. Were we trying to communicate? Or was he preparing me for what I was about to see. That little puppy had absolutely destroyed two low-hanging plants. Pink petals were scattered all over the ground. The plastic pots, now imprinted with puppy teeth marks, were turned upside down and laid on top of the mounds of potting soil. I guess he didn't like pink flowers. I could almost imagine him standing on his hind legs and rubbing his front paws together, as if to say, "so there!"

As part of my research activities, I had visited various web sites advertising dogsitting services, doggy day care centers, etc. One service which had particularly caught my attention had a link to an obedience trainer. This trainer was unique, as he focused on modifying behavior as well as on obedience training. I had planned to take my new puppy to some sort of group obedience training anyway, but the word "behavior" seemed to be screaming at me. I left a message for the trainer to call me. He returned my call just minutes after the breeder had called (my 72-hour return option was about to expire) to ask if I wanted to keep the puppy. At that moment, for some reason, I had a strange feeling that someone else had returned

4

Dusty, that someone else had said "No" when asked that question. I said, "Yes". He was mine. I couldn't give him up. Why? I don't know. I wondered if my puppy was crazy or suffering from abandonment issues. If only he could talk to me.

I couldn't reflect on these psychological issues very long. Dusty Thomas was running around the house, jumping and pulling on everything. He was "wild dog" again, and I couldn't get his attention for even a nanosecond. I sat down, put my head in my hands, and sobbed. I could call the breeder back. The phone rang. "Hello, Bettie? This is Duff Lueder." The trainer. "What can I do to help you and your puppy?" My story began. After talking with Duff for an hour, I felt better. He would come to my house (excuse me, "our" house now) and teach me how to communicate with my puppy.

I didn't keep a journal of our behavior modification program together (Dusty and me), but Dusty did. This book chronicles an ongoing conversation between Dusty (a dog) and Duffy (his trainer and our "behavior modifier"). This conversation is in the form of e-mails. It has been translated from DOG (which can be understood only by Dusty, other dogs, and Duffy) to HUMAN (which can be understood by the rest of us.) I, Dusty's handler, (also known as his "human mom") have read the e-mails but have not edited them. As dogs do not speak "human", Dusty hopes that after reading his e-mails to Duffy, you will be able to understand your dogs and communicate with them in a way that is more natural to them. We hope you enjoy the book.

March 3

TO: **Duffy**
FROM: **Puppy**
SUBJECT: **I've been dog-napped!**

Dear Duffy,

You used to be one of those policemen with a dog so I know you can help me. Today I was snatched from my home by a woman I don't know. She put me in her car and drove me a long way. She was strapped into her seat, but I didn't have a strap or even a little crate to ride in so I rambled all over the front seat. It was raining very hard, and those wiper things on the window made me very nervous and hyper. To protect myself, I

5

chewed on the woman's arm whenever I could get close to her. The trip was a terrible experience. Now she's holding me hostage at her house. My dog mother complained a little when she took me but didn't put up any real resistance, and my litter mates continued to play among themselves, oblivious to my situation. Therefore, I consider them to be accomplices to this crime. Here's what you need to know about me:

Facts

Name:	I don't know. This woman keeps saying these words: "Dusty Thomas". I think that might be my name, but I don't know.
Breed:	Welsh Terrier
Age:	14 weeks
Height:	??
Weight:	9 lbs
Color:	Black with touches of tan
Health:	My mouth hurts really bad because I'm teething.

This woman keeps throwing toys at me. I'm running as fast as I can, all through her house, and jumping on furniture to get out of the way. I never stop. If she gets near me, I run and sometimes bite at her. I throw tantrums too. I miss my litter mates and my step-sister Betsy (a Westie). Please come get me and take me home.

HELP ME!!!

A dog-napped WT

P.S. I'm very smart, but I'm just a baby and can't get myself out of this situation. I certainly can't TALK my way out of this situation!

Dusty thinks he's been dog-napped!

March 3

TO:	**Puppy**
FROM:	**Duffy**
SUBJECT:	**You have a new home!**

Dear Puppy,

Settle down. Don't panic or overreact. You have not been dog-napped. You just have a new home and now a new human mother. I have spoken with your new mom. She wants you to be happy and loves you very much, but she doesn't understand your hyperactive behavior and doesn't know how to communicate with you. She says she can't get your attention. She thinks you might be crazy. I don't think you are, but I'm coming over to your house tomorrow to help you and your new human mom understand each other and to help you get settled. The things you experienced in the car are due to the fact that you were thrust into a new set of circumstances, smells, and objects that you had never encountered before. These things are normal in your new surroundings, and your mom will learn how to properly condition you to handle them and understand that they will not harm you.

We will get started by setting up some "pack" rules for both of you to follow. These will be things that you will naturally understand, but at the same time will be natural for you to test. By helping your new human mom to set up these rules, she will in turn understand what motivates and instinctively governs your behavior.

We will start by giving you some fun jobs to do that will help you learn what your role is in your new pack and what is expected of you and what you can expect from your human mom in return. We will start a process where you will earn everything you get. This is something quite natural to your species, as in your view of the world, earning your status and place in your pack structure is the natural order of things. You already understand that if you do not earn something, you do not get it. That doesn't mean that more determined pack members (like you, Dusty) won't keep trying if they see new opportunities, however. ☺ So, we will have to help your new mom understand what your view of earning things is and what you expect for rewards when you do a good job. In your world, if one doesn't have to earn it, they are alpha leader. They get the best choices of food, places to sleep, toys, other play things, and affection, etc., first. Your species will naturally seek out this position of status until you are shown and understand that another leader is already in place. Sorry, Dusty, but this position will be reserved for your mom, but will be done with understanding, love, respect, and tough love when necessary, should you forget. ☺

Just between you and me, Dusty, we will make things real easy for you. In starting off learning how to fit into your new pack and get all the fun dog rewards you can handle, I will show you how to do a simple "sit" when your mom gives you the command, so that you show respect to her for her being the leader, and you in turn get to do and have the fun things that dogs love--food, toys, petting, and wonderful sounding tones of "Good boy, Dusty". Just don't tell your mom how really easy this is, ok? It will be our secret!

See you soon,
Duffy

P.S. Your name IS Dusty Thomas, but we will call you Dusty. OK?

March 4

TO:	**Duffy**
FROM:	**Dusty**

This secret stuff sounds like fun. I'm ready to play. I like food, toys, pettings, and "good boys". Don't worry about me telling mom. She doesn't listen to me anyway. She only listens to you. (Once I learn how to play this game, I can use this later for a new opportunity.)

Dusty

March 5

TO:	**Duffy**
FROM:	**Dusty**
SUBJECT:	**I am the leader of the pack!**

Dear Duffy,

I didn't really enjoy meeting you yesterday, but my mom did. You're supposed to be helping ME! I heard you talking to my mom for a very long time after you stuck me in my crate without saying a word to me and ignored me. You don't understand. I wanted ALL the attention, and I thought you were going to give me everything I wanted. I was having a great time trying to be leader of the pack (my mom doesn't know how to be, so I have to take over when I can't find a leader), but you stepped right in and took over my role. I heard you tell my mom I'm probably not crazy, but I am an alpha personality, dominant aggressive, and defiantly so, at that. It's not nice to call dogs names, Duffy. And ever since you left, my mom is calling, "Dusty, here!" I run to her every time, though, and I sit when she says "sit" (with a hand signal and that nice tone) because I love the treats, praise, and attention she gives me when I do. She also gives me lots of rubbin's when I do these things for her. I like my new mom, but she isn't always a very good leader and if I can't be the leader and have my way all the time, I'm not sure I want to stay. Are you going to teach her how to be a better leader?

Dusty

P.S. You're right. My name is Dusty. I know because my mom keeps saying, "Dusty, here!"

March 6

TO:	**Dusty**
FROM:	**Duffy**
SUBJECT:	**Sorry, your mom will be the leader!**

Dear Dusty,

I'm sorry you weren't happy about meeting me at first yesterday. I like you a lot, but I had to get your attention and the only way I could do that was to catch you in midair in the midst of one of your races through the house and carry you into your room and put you in your crate for some quiet time. You know from your dog mother that disrupting the pack is not acceptable. You're right about my not speaking a word to you. I never will when I put you in "timeout", which was what I was doing. You see, I want you to understand that if you cannot behave around the other pack members, then you can't be around them for a time. You are very social, and it is important that we socialize with "respect" for other pack members. Remember, I told you that the position of alpha leader would be reserved for your human mom and that in earning what you get, you will receive all the wonderful things that dogs love. For example, when I put you to bed and you are a good boy, I will say loving words to you. But, hey, you weren't in timeout very long--just a couple of minutes--and then after I let you out, I showed you that if you had manners (by coming when called and sitting), I would give you a treat and praise you for good pack behavior. I had to put you back into timeout a few minutes later, though, because you ran out and yanked on the vertical blinds with your teeth. We did this routine several times, as you recall, until you were a good boy when I let you out the last time. Also remember that I told you that this training would be done with understanding, love, respect, and tough love when needed, in case you forget. Sometimes it is necessary to repeat the teaching until you get it. Your species learns by mimic, repetition, and observation, so human leaders need to learn to be aware of this and that repetitions sometimes have to be varied due to the age and abilities of the individual dog.

Yours,
Duffy

Dusty really isn't in jail; he's just in "timeout"!

March 7

TO:	**Duffy**
FROM:	**Dusty**

OK! I'll try this thing! But it's normal for me to rule by biting, so if my mom doesn't learn how to be leader of our pack in a way I can understand, you know that I have to "naturally" take over.

Dusty

March 7

TO:	**Dusty**
FROM:	**Duffy**

I know it is hard to learn this all at once because your attention span is a bit short, but you'll make it, and your new mom and I will be patient with you. This timeout process and you learning how to interact with humans socially does not in any way cause you pain, discomfort or trauma. You instinctively know that separation from the pack means that your last behavior didn't fit in very well. But with humans, it is important that when you are allowed back with the pack, you are shown what IS acceptable and then given praise and rewards for your compliance. Sometimes humans forget this part, and that is where it can be very confusing for you and your species.

Yours,
Duffy

March 7

TO:	**Duffy**
FROM:	**Dusty**

I DIDN'T SAY IT HURT! I JUST DON'T LIKE BEING IGNORED!! I'll do my part as long as you make sure my mom does her part of this. If she forgets, can we put her in timeout? IT WON'T HURT HER EITHER!

Dusty

March 8

TO:	**Dusty**
From:	**Duffy**

I am going to teach your mom to be a good leader. You need some specific rules, young pup, and I'm going to help your mom establish and reinforce them in non-confrontational ways--you really do overreact when you're confronted. We are going to do some behavior modification on both you and your mom. ☺ You should know, though, that one of the things I will teach your mom is that SHE has to control time, space, objects, and height

13

when it comes to you to help you better understand what she means. She doesn't yet know that in your view of the world, if you can jump on it, bite it, or pee on it, you think you rule it. To be a good leader, she must never do anything for you unless you do something to earn it so that you know what is expected of you and you will know what to expect from her. So... no food, water, opening of doors, petting, playing or anything else unless you do something to earn it. Even something such as a simple "sit". Do it, and your mom will praise and reward you.

By the way, you are very smart, Dusty. I'm so proud of you for learning to run to your mom when she says, "Dusty here!" and for learning to sit so quickly. I know it's hard for you to concentrate when your teeth are aching, but you did it. Good boy! I'm also going to suggest some pet ora-gel, a special chew toy, and ice cubes for your aching teeth and gums. This should help you concentrate better.

See you next week! I'll teach you how to walk with your mom then.

Yours,
Duffy

P.S. I wasn't calling you names. I was labeling your behavior. You ARE a defiantly dominant aggressive puppy. You're also an alpha personality, which means you were probably the leader of the pack (your litter). As such, you were used to eating first (you pushed all your brothers and sisters out of the way to get to your mother) and bullied your way to being first in every other way. Your brothers and sisters deferred to you. So it was natural for you to try this at your new home. Your mom is learning to understand this so she can better communicate with you in ways you can understand.

Dusty, the term "dominance aggression" does not mean that you have serious behavioral problems. This is a common lump term that is a catchall for a number of specific aggressions, like territorial aggression, possession aggression, food aggression, as well as some others. Being more dominant does not mean you are bad or good, right or wrong. It means that you are more inclined to persistently test your environmental conditions (which includes humans, other dogs, and other pets) than the average dog. By the response you get from your testing, you then figure out what your role and place is within the group.

It is normal for living things to reach out and test their surroundings and environment. More assertive personalities just seem a bit pushier. ◉

Your mom will be learning that dealing with "dominance aggression" in training terms is what is called "alpha" or "leadership". Alpha does not mean one has to be the biggest or toughest. It simply means that one is "in charge". This can be done without being confrontational or intimidating. It comes down to respecting and understanding the motivations and signals that a dog receives about its behavior and that these things are based on a dog's instincts and perceptions of the world as s(he) views it—not as humans view it.

Dusty, it won't be enough for me to tell you that your new mom is your alpha leader. For you to understand, respect, and accept this, your mom must learn to demonstrate that she is your alpha leader while understanding, respecting, and accepting you for who you are with all the strengths and limitations of your species. It will be important for her to understand that you are not a furry little person and that you do not think or communicate like a human. You think and respond to the world through the mind and eyes of a dog, which is truly very special. This will open up the doors to communication and you and your new mom will have fewer misunderstandings.

Dusty is ready to compete for the position of Alpha Leader!

March 10

TO:	**Duffy**
FROM:	**Dusty**
SUBJECT:	**She tricked me!**

Dear Duffy,

Dusty here. It isn't fair. I don't get to just do my own thing anymore. My mom squirts water in my face (which really startles me) when I'm demanding something, jumping on or biting her, and then throws me a toy. By the time I grab the toy and run around the room with it, I have forgotten what I was trying to demand of her. This part is really a lot of fun and the treat she gives me is nice, but I know SHE TRICKED ME. Darn it! I want to be in control!

I do like the peanut butter she spreads on that hollow rubber toy. It tastes so yummy, but I'm so preoccupied with it that I don't notice that she puts me in my crate and leaves for awhile. By the time I realize she's gone, there's no point in throwing a tantrum. (Tantrums are fun!!!) SHE TRICKED ME!

Hurry back. We need to talk.

Dusty

P.S. My teeth feel better. Mom sprinkles water on a knotted towel and puts it in the freezer until it is very cold and then gives it to me. I like to chew on it, and it makes my mouth feel better. She also noticed that I love eating ice cubes so she made me some special ones--they taste like chicken soup. Mom is not all that bad. We just disagree on a lot of stuff. Maybe I'll stay.

March 11

TO:	**Dusty**
FROM:	**Duffy**
SUBJECT:	**Wrong!**

Dear Dusty,

The world is not fair, and you are not going to be in control. Your mom is not tricking you. She is modifying your behavior--and her own behavior too, for that matter, so as you learn more about each other, the two of you can have more fun together. Sounds to me like it is working and it sounds like you really do like it.

Your new mom is also learning to ignore the negative and reinforce the positive in your behavior. The squirt bottle (which you are not supposed to like) is meant to "startle" you when you are being pack disruptive so that your mom can then show you what kind of behavior you CAN DO that is acceptable. Biting, jumping, and pawing, although normal in your world and interactions with your litter mates, is not pleasant to humans; so all the fun stuff your mom rewards you with for doing a good job are helping to direct your behavior and interactions with humans into a more pleasant experience for you and the humans you encounter.

These things that your mom is showing you to do, like going in your crate for a time when she leaves and fetching fun toys instead of biting or jumping, are to let you know that these are normal everyday events and are part of your role and job in your new pack. You are coming along very well, and you will be just fine.

See you in two days.

Duffy

P.S. Did you remember to thank your mom for the ice cubes?

P.P.S. By the way, Dusty, you are getting to be a big boy and it's time for you to go see the doggie doctor, who is called a "Vet". This will be a new experience for you. Don't worry. I've already prepared your mom for this, and she'll make sure everything is ok and take care of you so you need not be frightened. Be sure to let me know what you think.

March 11

| TO: | **Duffy** |
| **FROM:** | **Dusty** |

WAIT A MINUTE! SHE's TAKING ME SOMEWHERE?! IN THAT CAR WITH THOSE WIPER THINGS?! FORGET IT! I'M NOT GOING! YOU CAN'T MAKE ME! I'LL RUN AND YOU CAN'T CATCH ME!

March 11

| TO: | **Dusty** |
| **FROM:** | **Duffy** |

It's ok. Be calm. It won't be the same. Remember, we taught her to put you in a crate for your safety so you won't get bounced around in the car. Mom will give you a special toy or treat to keep you occupied so even if it's raining, the wipers won't get you.

March 12

TO:	**Duffy**
FROM:	**Dusty**
SUBJECT:	**The Vet**

Dear Duffy,

You were right! Today my mom took me to the vet to get shots. It was so scary, I could hardly deal with it. The first lady I met introduced herself as Auntie Jane (Mom says she's your wife, so I'm going to call you "Uncle Duffy") and gave me a treat when I sat. I liked her, but I wasn't sure if I should trust her or anyone else. She picked me up and put me down on this cold metal table. I tried to get away. I ran and ran but got nowhere. I couldn't even stand up on that slippery table. I would just go "splat" on my tummy. Auntie Jane put her arms around me like a fence to keep me from going head first off the table. Another lady was trying to take my temperature in a very private part of my body. I DIDN'T LIKE IT! YOU DIDN'T TELL ME ABOUT THAT PART!! Then the doc came in. By this time, I was really hyper and also on the verge of exhaustion. He picked me up too. I wiggled and wiggled and fought, trying to get away. He had a very firm hold on me. He put me up against his shoulder and petted me with long strokes and kept saying, "calm, calm". For some reason, I felt a little better. He gave me some shots so I wouldn't get sick. They didn't hurt. He put a microchip in my shoulder so in case I get lost, I can be found. That didn't hurt either. But, hey, I wanted out of there. I was not in control, and you know how uncomfortable I am with that. My mom took me out to the car, put me in my crate, and I crashed. When I woke up, I was home with mom. Not a bad place to be.

Yours,
Dusty

Dusty looks a little "wiped out" after his trip to the vet!

March 12

TO:	**Dusty**
FROM:	**Duffy**
SUBJECT:	**The Vet**

Dear Dusty,

Going to the doctor can be a bit stressful for us humans too. ☺ I know that it must be hard to understand all the new things that happen to you there (both the comfortable and uncomfortable), but it is sometimes necessary to help you feel better and prevent you from getting sick. Going at least once a year to get checked will help you live a long and wonderful life in your new home.

Because it was something new, I know it really tired you out. But each time you go, you will notice that wonderful things happen as well, and the new people are very interested in you and want you to be happy and healthy just like your human mom. Don't worry; it is not a bad thing.

Yours,
Duffy

P.S. Yes, you can call me "Uncle Duffy".

Dusty is resting after his trip to the vet.

March 13

TO:	Uncle Duffy
FROM:	Dusty
SUBJECT:	I want food---now!!!

Dear Uncle Duffy,

Dusty here. #!@#! My mom has taken my food away. She sets it down only twice a day. I liked eating whenever I wanted to. This is too much discipline! What difference does it make when (or if) I eat?

Yours,
Dusty

P.S. Oh, I forgot to tell you. Remember that big crate you put me in for the 2-minute warning that you call a timeout? You know, the one I also sleep in at night? It's big and spacious. Since there's so much room, I just do my potties in there too--in a corner. I don't sleep in it, but, geez, does it upset Mom! She always pushes me outside when I do this. I don't get it. What's the problem here? I didn't potty in HER house. I think MOM is crazy!

Dusty

March 13

TO:	Dusty
FROM:	Uncle Duffy
SUBJECT:	Your food will be available twice a day for 15-20 minutes at a time. Eat up!

Dear Dusty,

Take it easy, little pup. Two things are going on here. First, because you were eating anytime you wanted, essentially all the time, you were going potty all the time too. You're a puppy, and your bowels and bladder are small and not regulated yet like an adult dog. Second, we want you to go potty less and OUTSIDE the house. Outside your crate too. I understand why you potty in your crate. There's plenty of room so you do it and get away from it. I'll suggest to your mom that she get you a smaller crate or get a divider for this one until you get a little bigger. It will be nice and cozy and you can curl up in it like you would curl up in a den if you lived in the wild.

Yours,
Uncle Duffy

P.S. By the way, your mom is not crazy. Neither are you! (I don't know if I ever told you.)

March 14

TO:	**Uncle Duffy**
FROM:	**Dusty**
SUBJECT:	**My friend's parents rub her nose in her own potty!**

Dear Uncle Duffy,

Can you believe this? Today when Mom and I were walking so I could go potty outside, I met another little dog. Now she's my friend, and she says if she has an accident inside her house, her parents rub her nose in her own potty!! Why would they do that? She is just a little puppy. My mom never did that to me. You don't agree with this practice, do you???

Yours,
Dusty

March 14

TO:	**Dusty**
FROM:	**Uncle Duffy**
SUBJECT:	**NO!**

Dear Dusty,

I feel bad for your friend, Dusty. Under no circumstances should this be done to a dog. Her parents are not thinking about how much more sensitive a dog's nose is than theirs. I'm sure they don't rub their toddler's noses in their soiled pants. This is a barbaric practice. It is important to remember that if your friend has an accident in the house, it is exactly that. An accident! Not something she did deliberately or out of spite. After all, your friend can't let herself out. Regulating diet and having a proper, consistent feeding and watering schedule, consistently taking your friend outside to go potty in a particular place, praising her when she goes, and providing a crate or outside kennel run for her when she cannot be monitored, will help prevent and eliminate these "accidents". There are three times when dogs will have house-training accidents: 1) after they eat, 2) after they sleep, and 3) after they play. If these situations are monitored by the human leader, house training will work without undue stress on your friend or her human family. Feel free to share my response with your friend, and tell her we love her.

Yours,
Uncle Duffy

March 16

TO:	**Uncle Duffy**
FROM:	**Dusty**
SUBJECT:	**Walking on the left side of mom**

Dear Uncle Duffy,

Dusty here. This walking stuff that you taught me last time is really weird. My mom has four legs, but she only walks on two of them. That's weird. I can do that too, but I could never walk as far as she does on just my hind legs. Sometimes she takes big steps and other times she takes small steps. It's hard to walk with her. I have figured out, though, that when she pats her left leg, steps out with her left foot, and says, "heel", she wants me to walk right beside her. When I do that right, she uses the "sit" hand signal and says, "Dusty, sit." Then she gives me a yummy treat (different from the ones she gives me inside the house). Then she pats her left leg again, steps out with her left foot, says, "heel", and we do the same thing again. Kinda weird, but, hey, I can play this game!

Thanks for the new necklace. I like the larger links--it makes the necklace masculine. It's very comfortable. I think it's magic, though, because when I walk ahead of mom or move to her right side (I know I'm supposed to walk on her left), the necklace grips me--just like my dog mother did when I was still with my litter. I then put myself right back where I'm supposed to be. Mom likes my hands-free leash too. She says it's comfortable wearing it like a shoulder-strapped purse (whatever that is), and her hands are free to shake hands with the neighbors. I don't get to shake hands with the neighbors (boy, how I would like to jump on them and lick them in the face). I have to sit and let them pat me on the head. Only thing I didn't like about learning to walk with mom is that I want to sniff around on my own ALL the time. How else can I tell who's been in the neighborhood?

Yours,
Dusty

March 17

TO:	**Dusty**
FROM:	**Uncle Duffy**
SUBJECT:	**Congratulations!**

Dear Dusty,

Of course you can play this game! Practice makes perfect, and I'm glad to hear you are practicing. More important, your practice should be fun! I knew you would like the "necklace"--it's called a "collar", Dusty. It, along with the leash your mom uses, is designed for her to maintain control of the "space" you two are in so that she can focus her attention on what it is she is teaching you, all the while providing a means of keeping you in an area of protection from things that might harm you.

Don't worry, Dusty. While you are on your walks, there will be special times and places that your mom will let you sniff around and check out who has been in the neighborhood. But remember, alpha leader chooses those times and places because more often than not, in the human world, some places are not as safe for you to just do your dog thing. So be patient with your mom while she is learning, and she will be patient with you while you are.

Just keep practicing and be a good boy until I see you again.

Yours,
Uncle Duffy

Dusty thinks he's an "angel" because he is learning how to obey his mom's commands.

March 18

TO:	**Uncle Duffy**
FROM:	**Dusty**
SUBJECT:	**My mom doesn't know how to play!**

Dear Uncle Duffy,

I want to go back to my dog mother. She let me play with my litter mates—you know, chew on them, nip at them, roll and play. My human mother just won't let me play with her like that. She's no fun! She won't let me attack the TV box either. I love to watch the TV box, but sometimes I get so excited that I just...ATTACK, especially when there are animals in that box or people are dancing. Cartoon characters really bug me. I hate them. They are so squirrelly.

Dusty

March 18

TO:	**Dusty**
FROM:	**Uncle Duffy**
SUBJECT:	**Let's teach your mom how to play—with you!**

Dear Dusty,

I know your dog mother allowed you to jump on, play bite, and wrestle your litter mates, but that is because this is normal interaction and communication among dogs. One problem that we as humans have is that our skin cannot take the pawing, nipping, or biting without us being injured. Pain to humans (just like with dogs) is very uncomfortable and stressful and can cause overreactions out of frustration and anger. So, I'm going to teach your human mom to play with you in a way that works well with dogs and humans and is something you particularly really like. You, like other dogs, like to chase things and be chased. So, I will teach your mom to throw toys or balls for you to chase, catch, and even retrieve. When you bring the toy back to your mom, she will praise you and throw it for you again. This way, you won't accidentally hurt your mom by play biting and jumping and she won't get angry and misunderstand that you only wanted to play, not be disrespectful.

27

Duff Lueder and Bettie LaDuke

When you see animals on TV, it is normal for you to want to interact with them because you understand them. But Dusty, the TV animals and other humans that you see in the box are what we call pictures we can make move. Like memories you can actually see. They won't harm you or take your toys. Jumping at the box may hurt you so your mom will redirect your attention with something you like and CAN do.

Be a good boy and see you soon.

Yours,
Uncle Duffy

Dusty likes to run, romp, wrestle, and play!

March 20

TO:	**Uncle Duffy**
FROM:	**Dusty**
SUBJECT:	**I'm frustrated about something!**

Dear Uncle Duffy,

I am just so frustrated! I want to see what's on top of tables and counters, and the only way I can do that is to jump. I can jump really high! My mom hates for me to jump and squirts me in the face with that water bottle. I don't like it so I mouth her and argue with her. I don't mean to hurt her; I'm just trying to argue my case. But Mom says my teeth are so sharp they cut her arm. I can't help it that my teeth are sharp—they are just baby teeth—but they are very sharp because they are my only means of protection. My mom doesn't understand that. We are really having some huge battles over these things. Sometimes I get so frustrated that I just hurl myself against the cabinets in the kitchen. This starts a small war with my mom, and we both go to pieces. What should I do?

Dusty

P.S. My mom also doesn't understand that I HATE SURPRISES! She suddenly turns on noisy things—the garbage disposal, the vacuum cleaner. That drives me crazy! I can't help it. I just go berserk!

March 21

TO:	**Dusty**
FROM:	**Uncle Duffy**
SUBJECT:	**Stop it right now!**

Dear Dusty,

I'm sorry you're feeling frustrated—your teething is contributing to that—but you don't get to jump on anything. If there's something on top of tables or counters that your mom wants you to have, she will give it to you. Period. Mouthing is never allowed. You must learn these two rules right now: 1) you must have all four feet on the floor at all times; and 2) your teeth must never touch a human. Meanwhile, I'll explain to your mom that she needs to redirect your attention away from things

29

you're not supposed to have by startling you with a squirt of water and then immediately redirecting you by then tossing you a toy to fetch. Grab the toy and run around the house until you're no longer frustrated. Your mom will reward you handsomely when you do this. You're going to have to work at this because you're a pretty hyper and intense guy, but you can do it. Your mom will also have to be very consistent in her response to you until you catch on. Good luck.

Noisy things that your mom turns on, like the garbage disposal and the vacuum cleaner, are normal things in your new environment that she needs to get you conditioned to. They will not harm you but are a part of your new world. In this training process, I will teach your mom to give you something interesting and fun to do in a different area of the house when these noisy things are used until you can get used to them comfortably. It will be ok!

Yours,
Uncle Duffy

March 22

TO:	**Uncle Duffy**
FROM:	**Dusty**
SUBJECT:	**I have lots of fun under the bed!**

Dear Uncle Duffy,

I've found a really fun spot to play—under my mom's bed. It's a great place to escape from her too. She puts things under the bed. There's a plastic box with something in it. I can't open that box. There's also a motor of some kind that makes a noise when I step or lay on a button. I don't like the noise so I bark and really fuss at it. When I move or take my paw off the button, it's quiet again. Today my mom started making her bed (I never make mine), and she started laughing, laughing, laughing. One side of the bed was completely flat. She said, "Dusty, you must have had your paw on the air bed button!" I don't know what that means, but mom thought it was funny. I wonder if I can make her laugh again!

Dusty

Dusty loves to play under the bed!

March 22

TO: **Dusty**
FROM: **Uncle Duffy**
SUBJECT: **Fun under the bed**

Dear Dusty,

Like with new human babies and toddlers, human parents enjoy watching their young dogs go through discovery. It is healthy and, yes, will at times make your human mom laugh. I'm sure as you grow and develop there will be many more things you do that will put a smile on your mom's face.

Yours,
Uncle Duffy

March 23

TO:	**Uncle Duffy**
FROM:	**Dusty**

Dusty here. I am getting to really like this love and bonding thing, especially if I get to play under the bed! I really like it when Mom is happy.

Dusty

March 23

TO:	**Dusty**
FROM:	**Uncle Duffy**

Dusty, this will probably always be the case, as long as your activity is not something harmful to you or others. Human/canine interaction is supposed to be one of joy, love, bonding, and growth. Learning about one another and appreciating the love of life is what our relationship with you (our dog) is supposed to be all about.

Because of this special developing bond between dogs and humans of wanting to please each other and make each other laugh and be happy, I'm going to share with you (and with those who read this book) something a good friend of mine wrote and sent to me. You will see it on our web site and in our instruction. It was written by a very knowledgeable dog training expert. Her name is Candy Wisnieski. She is the Chairman of Obedience Training, Ramapo Kennel Club; Board Member, The Collie Club of Northern New Jersey; Member, Collie Club of America & the Collie Health Foundation of New Jersey. Here it is:

Dusty laughs and makes his mom laugh too!

MY LOVING CONTRACT WITH YOU, MY DOG

* I (your human leader) agree to take you (my dog) under my care and protection!

* I will love and respect you, and you will love and respect me!

* As I am the leader of the dog/handler team, it is my responsibility to learn how to properly lead you!

* I will never ask you to do something you can't do. I promise to understand that you, as the dog, are a different species--with your own special language, instincts, motivations, and intelligence, which are different from mine. As the human leader, it is my responsibility to know your abilities and limitations at any given moment and to have expectations that fit them. It is my responsibility to learn how your mind works, to learn how you grow and develop, and to learn how to properly communicate with you in a way you naturally can understand. It is my responsibility to prepare you for your future life with me!

* I will praise you lavishly when you do something positive-----EVERY TIME!

* I will take the responsibility to make sure you are successful. When you do something I find unacceptable, I will understand that you are not to blame. It is because you were either INSUFFICIENTLY TRAINED, INSUFFICIENTLY SOCIALIZED, and/or INSUFFICIENTLY SUPERVISED

* I will try not to lose my temper and yell at you, and I will NEVER strike you in anger. I will sometimes correct and redirect you for errors, but will not exact punishment. For it is my responsibility to figure out a way to repeat the teaching so that you understand it better; practice it more; and/or I will rearrange your environment and schedule so that you are less likely to make a mistake. To best do this, I will not put you in a situation that you are too unprepared or too immature to handle!

* I will protect you from the dangers of my environment.

* I will see that you get good veterinary care and will provide you with a healthy lifestyle!

* I will give you the opportunity to get enough exercise!

* I will spend the time it takes to train you and take you places to socialize you!

* I will feed, groom, and bathe you, as well as cuddle, pet, and play with you!

* In return for all that I am responsible to do for you as your dog parent, I know that I will receive the immeasurable gifts that have been freely given for generations by your species: **unconditional love, your joy of life, your lack of criticism, your tolerance and forgiveness, your sense of humor, and your patience with my faults.**

With all my love,

Your Human Leader

Thank you, Dusty.
Uncle Duffy

March 24

TO:	**Uncle Duffy**
FROM:	**Dusty**
SUBJECT:	**That Loving Contract**

Dear Uncle Duffy,

No problem with the contract. I'll keep my part of the deal. My species always has!

Yours,
Dusty

March 24

TO: **Dusty**
FROM: **Uncle Duffy**
SUBJECT: **That Loving Contract**

Dear Dusty,

Your mom will keep her part of the deal too! She loves you too much not to.

Yours,
Uncle Duffy

Dusty and his mom

March 28

TO:	**Uncle Duffy**
FROM:	**Dusty**
SUBJECT:	**I don't want to "stay"!**

Dear Uncle Duffy,

Dusty here. Isn't sitting and heeling enough to earn food, water, praises, etc.? (I'd still rather DEMAND them, but I seldom get away with that kind of behavior anymore.) Now my mom expects me to stay in one spot while she goes into another room, takes something out of the oven, or whatever. Will you tell her how silly this is?

Thanks,
Dusty

March 28

TO:	**Dusty**
FROM:	**Uncle Duffy**
SUBJECT:	**You have to "stay".**

Dear Dusty,

Of course you have to learn to stay in one spot—for as long as your mom wants you to stay, as long as she knows your limits (and she does). You have to sit and stay while your mom greets people when you're walking. Then you can greet them politely and get all sorts of praise, treats, and love. You have to sit and stay while she fumbles with the key trying to unlock the door to the house. You have to stay while she gets things out of the pantry or closets. You can't just be running and jumping all the time. You have to be a gentleman too. Do it. It's not so bad. It's worth the yummy treats, praise, and loving mom provides, isn't it? Remember when I told you this stuff was really easy? You can do it! Besides, it is your new job!

Yours,
Uncle Duffy

March 29

TO:	**Uncle Duffy**
FROM:	**Dusty**
SUBJECT:	**Sleepover**

Dear Uncle Duffy,

Mom says I'm going to stay with you and Auntie Jane (she lives with you?) for a few days while she goes on a trip. Mom says you have some dogs, some birds, and a cat. Wow! A real pack! See you in a couple days.

Yours,
Dusty

March 29

TO:	**Dusty**
FROM:	**Uncle Duffy**
SUBJECT:	**Get ready for the sleepover!**

Dear Dusty,

Auntie Jane and I are looking forward to you coming to our home for your sleepover while your mom is away. I told our dogs that you were coming and they, too, are excited about your visit. I told them that you were not used to being around other dogs a lot but that you liked having a good time. They advised that they would help you fit in but that there was a certain pecking order and set of pack rules that you would have to learn. They indicated that they would show you the ropes and how to have some real dog fun. Dusty, I know you are not sure what the pack rules mean, but it is important to know that dog packs have a certain hierarchy and this must always be respected. The dominant female, which at our house is "Kahlua" (an Australian Shepherd), is in charge of the internal workings of the pack. She is female alpha leader. Next in the pecking order is "Nitro" (our Standard Poodle). He is the dominant male and is in charge of the territorial perimeters of the pack, and when everyone is outside, he is the boss. Next in the pecking order is our other female, "Pickles" (our Jack Russell Terrier). Then next is another male Standard Poodle, "Drake"; and last, but not least, is our female Black Labrador, "Brita". You will be last in the pecking order, Dusty, unless the other dogs in their individual positions say it is ok for you to be above them in station. As human leaders, Auntie Jane and I will have to make sure that these rules are adhered to so that everyone has fun.

With the exception of Nitro, all of our dogs love to chase things and be chased. It is called the "Git em" game! Nitro likes to watch and supervise and make sure nothing gets out of hand. ☺ He feels it is his job to watch out for everyone when they are outside. So, you will have a lot of fun and learn more socialization skills while you are with us.

Yours,
Uncle Duffy

Kahlua—the female alpha leader

Nitro—the "outside" boss

Pickles

Drake

Brita

Me—Dusty—at the bottom of the pack. Hmmm!

March 29

TO: **Uncle Duffy**
FROM: **Dusty**

Oh great! First you tell me Mom is leader of the pack, then you and Auntie Jane are leaders of the pack, and now you tell me Kahlua, Nitro, Drake, Pickles, and Brita are pack leaders over me in their social order. I understand how this works. You say I'll have a lot of fun. I believe you, but I STILL WANT TO BE LEADER!

Dusty

March 30

TO:	**Uncle Duffy and Auntie Jane**
FROM:	**Dusty**
SUBJECT:	**The Sleepover**

Dear Uncle Duffy and Auntie Jane,

Thank you for taking care of me while my mom was out of town. I learned a little about pack hierarchy as soon as you introduced me to your dogs. Nitro rolled me, remember? It was kinda fun, but I got his message that he was boss instead of me. I kept trying, though, didn't I?

I'm sorry I attacked human ankles every time someone walked by. Now I know why Auntie Jane called me a piranha puppy. (My mom told me what it meant. I laughed when she told me, but she said it wasn't funny. She said I was demanding attention.)

I had a blast!
Dusty

P.S. Next time I will be more mature, I promise. Tell Nitro, please.

Dusty had a blast at the sleepover—he made new friends!

March 30

TO:	**Uncle Duffy**
FROM:	**Dusty**
SUBJECT:	**I had to dig up the flowers!**

Dear Uncle Duffy,

What am I supposed to do? There was a field mouse in my mom's flower bed and I caught it. No sooner had I smelled it than I was digging as fast as I could to get it out of there. You should have seen me. Mud was flying everywhere! I caught the mouse, and I had a great time doing it. I was so proud! I took the mouse in the house to show Mom. She didn't exactly react the way I expected, but she didn't get mad. She did dump my mouse somewhere, though. But when she saw my diggings, wow! She was so upset with me. Why? I did a great job protecting her. I'm so confused. I don't want to stay here anymore.

Dusty

"Look closely and you can see the mouse in my mouth. I had to dig up Mom's flowers to catch it!"

April 1

TO:	**Dusty**
FROM:	**Uncle Duffy**
SUBJECT:	**It will be ok. I'll talk to Mom!**

Dear Dusty,

I'm sure your mom very much appreciated you rescuing her from the mouse. On the other hand, humans can get a bit touchy when flower beds and yards get dug up. I will explain to your mom that it is natural for a dog to dig, as the smell of fresh earth is stimulating to you and as you are a terrier (who specializes in catching and dispatching rodents), that this was not only fun, but instinctive. It might be a good idea to have your mom either restrict you from getting to the flowers or move them

48

to a new location. This way you will not be put into a situation that you (instinctively or because of your maturity) can't handle. This can best prevent misunderstandings and unintentional overreactions from both you and your mom.

I will explain to her that there are a lot of dog behaviors and instincts that (although not acceptable to us as humans) are normal in a dog's view of the world. When these behaviors manifest themselves, they are not done out of spite or vindictiveness towards us as humans, but in the natural course of a dog's life. Understanding of these things by humans will help us better deal with and help our dogs to not be put into situations where they can make mistakes. This is because "mistakes" are exactly what these behaviors are. Nothing more, and nothing less. It should always be in the back of the human leader's mind that it is not a natural act for a dog (domestic or otherwise) to live and interact within the human social structure. As a different species, although subordinate to humans, it is not a dog's responsibility to understand humans, but rather the human's responsibility to show understanding and teach the dog how to fit in. Dog parenting and leadership is the ability to anticipate and prevent unacceptable behaviors through redirection so that these misunderstandings and communication problems don't occur.

See you soon.
Uncle Duffy

Uncle Duffy arrived to console Dusty.

April 4

TO:	**Uncle Duffy**
FROM:	**Dusty**
SUBJECT:	**My friend sheds just terribly!**

Dear Uncle Duffy,

Dusty here. Guess what? I have a new friend--a black lab. I love for her to come over to play, but Mom says she has to stay outside. I can't bring her into my room because Mom says she leaves hair all over the place. I don't mind, but my mom hates it! I don't know why her hair comes out like it does. Mine doesn't. Is there anything you can do about her shedding? Some sort of behavior modification?

Yours,
Dusty

April 5

TO: **Dusty**
FROM: **Uncle Duffy**
SUBJECT: **There's no behavior to modify, but here are some things to try.**

Dear Dusty,

Your hair doesn't come out like your friend's because as a terrier, you have "hair", not "fur," so you shed differently and very little in comparison to other breeds. The first thing you should do is suggest she be checked out by a vet for health problems such as skin problems or dermatitis. If these things aren't the problem, it could be the food she is eating. There are all kinds of food on the market today. Some are better than others--better in the sense they are more palatable to dogs. In other words, what goes in (or most of it) stays in, which is healthier for the dog.

A lot of skin problems occur from within, and there are a lot of good supplements available that deal with various skin conditions. One that has had some recent positive results has been, believe it or not, sardines or fish in oil. I know you love sardines, Dusty. The fish and oil combination contains folic acid, which works to counter certain types of dermatitis conditions such as hot spots and even flea saliva sensitivity. A can of sardines in oil, for example, can be put on your friend's food once or twice a week. Also, tell her mom to avoid excessive bathing, as it can remove certain necessary skin oils, which in turn can cause itching.

Your friend will shed a couple times a year due to weather conditions, which is quite normal. The itching, however, isn't normal. Again, I suggest a vet check to eliminate any skin type health conditions and then follow through with a good dietary plan and good recommended food from her vet. Hope this helps. I'll be happy to talk with your friend's mom and dad if you can arrange it.

Yours,
Uncle Duffy

Dusty's friend Abby

Dusty's friend Bailey

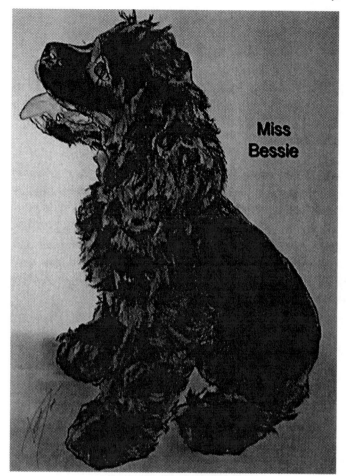

Dusty's friend Bessie

April 7

TO: **Uncle Duffy**
FROM: **Dusty**

Wow! I'm going to try to pull out some of my hair so I can get some sardines!

Dusty

April 6

TO:	**Uncle Duffy**
FROM:	**Dusty**
SUBJECT:	**My friend does #1 in the house when someone pets her.**

Dear Uncle Duffy,

Dusty here. I told you about my friend the black lab (the one that sheds so badly). Well, now I have another friend, a pretty female about one year old, and I really like her to come over to my house to play. My mom doesn't like her to come into my room, though, because she does #1 right on the floor when someone pets her. She just gets so excited, and she's so cute that all the humans want to pet her. This is pretty embarrassing for her (and for me—she's MY friend), but she just won't stop doing it. Can we modify her behavior somehow?

Yours,
Dusty

P.S. This one is really important to me because she is my first girlfriend.

April 7

TO:	**Dusty**
FROM:	**Uncle Duffy**
SUBJECT:	**There could be multiple reasons for this.**

Dear Dusty,

I can tell that you are experiencing "puppy love" and that this case is very important to you so I'm answering you right away. Suggest these things to your girlfriend's mom and dad: First, take her to a vet to make sure there isn't anything wrong with her. Second, don't leave water out for her all the time.

It sounds like she gets so excited to greet people that it just sort of shakes loose. Well, tell her parents to try not letting her greet people on her own. Let her meet people on leash only, and make her sit to greet them. (Just like we taught you to greet people, Dusty, even though you don't have this problem.)

If her parents take charge of who, what, when, and where she meets people and when she gets pettings, they will have the problem under control. When she gets excited and does #1, her parents must take her outside immediately, praising her when she relieves herself outside. Tell them not to scold her for these "accidents" around people, because she could misunderstand what she's being scolded for. They don't want her to be afraid of meeting new people.

I truly feel your girlfriend will grow out of this in time. After all, she is still a puppy. Some puppies, when overly excited, relieve themselves and don't even realize they do it, so it's important that when she gets pettings, it is done slowly and in a calm voice. This and the sitting on leash will help prevent her from getting overly excited and having an accidental bladder episode.

Good luck and let me know how it goes.

Yours,
Uncle Duffy

April 8

TO:	**Uncle Duffy**
FROM:	**Dusty**
SUBJECT:	**Love?!**

Dear Uncle Duffy,

Dusty here. I AM NOT IN ANY KIND OF LOVE!@#!

Dusty

Love?!

April 9

TO:	**Dusty**
FROM:	**Uncle Duffy**
SUBJECT:	**Would you LIKE to be in love?**

Dear Dusty,

I want you to meet Morgan. Morgan is a beautiful three-year-old Lhasa Apso. She has a great personality—now. When I first met her, she was incorrigible—much like you were when I first met you. She barked constantly and ran around the house, biting anyone in site—her human parents and the other two dogs that lived with her. No one could sneeze, cough, wash dishes, cook, play the stereo, use the phone, use surround sound for entertainment, or even talk without her viciously attacking them. She was so unmanageable that her vet told her mother she was crazy and should take tranquilizers or even be put to sleep!

I've known Morgan for over a year now, and she is much more settled and very sweet. She gets to go places with her human mom and dad and likes people and other dogs—like you. She likes to do exciting things—like riding a motor bike with her parents. She thinks she's a "biker babe" now. I think you two are very compatible. I've attached a picture.

Yours,
Uncle Duffy

Dusty's friend Morgan

April 9

TO:	**Uncle Duffy**
FROM:	**Dusty**
SUBJECT:	**The Biker Babe**

Dear Uncle Duffy,

I WOULD like to meet Morgan. She's pretty!

I'll get my mom to buy me a leather jacket. I saw some at a pet store. Then maybe you can arrange for me to go for a ride on the bike with Morgan. Afterwards, we can swap some stories and chew on some rawhide.

Dusty

Dusty's friend Cessna

April 9

TO:	**Uncle Duffy**
FROM:	**Dusty**

SUBJECT: **This female dog is totally dependent on her mom and won't go walking with any other members of her family.**

Dear Uncle Duffy,

Dusty here. I have a friend who is a two-year-old Lhasa mix who will only let her mom walk her outside. If her mom's not at home, only then will she walk with her dad and her human brothers and sisters. (Sounds like a manipulator to me, Uncle Duffy.) Anyway, this is very inconvenient for her mom. Is there any way to get her to cooperate with the other family members? She drags on the lead, squats, or just doesn't go potty to show she's unhappy.

Dusty

April 10

TO:	**Dusty**
FROM:	**Uncle Duffy**
SUBJECT:	**Your friend needs some tough love!**

Dear Dusty,

It sounds to me like your friend is a very smart little dog, who has taught her family well.

If this truly is a concern to her parents, they need to "tough love" her. You've experienced some "tough love" yourself, haven't you, Dusty? As long as she gets away with this behavior, she will continue to do this. The "tough love" part of this process is that her human mom needs to stop walking her until she walks well with the others in her family. It will take a great deal of her mom's will power to not give in to her, but it will be worth it in the long run.

When the others walk her, they must go, even if she balks. Just keep walking until she gets up and walks on her own. The first time will be the worst! She will whine, cry, roll, and do other silly things to get them to stop so she can be with her mom. They have to "tough love" her just like sometimes she has to "tough love" them. In this process, however, it is advisable to have a skilled trainer show each new handler how to ignore the negative and reinforce the positive by focusing your friend's attention on something she really likes, such as a very yummy treat. She then gets this treat when she walks without being disruptive. This needs to be done in a patient manner so that the stress your friend feels toward this new situation is gradually decreased and she realizes that this is a normal event that will not harm her but, rather, reward her. It will also be important that her human leaders be enthusiastic and have fun during this time. Enthusiasm, like a smile, is contagious. ☺

Her mom must remember that she is the mommy, not the dog. That means her mom is alpha leader! She must be firm, fair, loving and, most of all, consistent. Your friend will then stop this behavior and everyone will win.

Yours,
Uncle Duffy

April 11

| TO: | **Uncle Duffy** |
| FROM: | **Dusty** |

I remember! My mom learned how to be leader of our pack, so maybe I can get her to talk to my friend's mom and tell her how to make this better.

Dusty

Dusty's friends Much and Too Much

Dusty's friend Oba

April 11

TO:	**Uncle Duffy**
FROM:	**Dusty**
SUBJECT:	**This dog is really aggressive—worse than me!**

Dear Uncle Duffy,

Dusty here. About a month ago, one of my human neighbors found a dog. He's about three years old and is a cross between a Fox Terrier and a Jack Russell Terrier (yea, terriers!!!). His name is Russell. He wasn't tagged or registered. (I AM! I even have a chip on my shoulder—a microchip!). My neighbor brought him home and found the owner about a week later when he took Russell out for a run. Can you believe Russell's owner hadn't even looked for him??? His owner had encouraged Russell to bark at other people and animals because he wanted him to guard his tools. Russell ran away a lot (I would have too, Uncle Duffy). He didn't take good care of Russell and told my neighbor he didn't want Russell anymore. Poor Russell. My human neighbor kept him and gives him lots of love and attention. I tried to play with him, but he is very aggressive and we don't have any fun. He is especially aggressive towards human strangers. He barks at his parents' friends (who even live in the same house as he does), and he is a menace to everyone—cyclists, children, old men and women. He charges at them and tries to bite them!! He has been sad and frustrated almost all his life, and he doesn't trust anyone—not even me. What can we do to help him?

Dusty

Dusty's friend Elsa

Dusty's friends Ebony, Sassy, and Ariel

April 12

TO: **Dusty**
FROM: **Uncle Duffy**
SUBJECT: **It's not his fault!   Russell needs patience and consistency in his life.**

Dear Dusty,

I'm so sorry to hear about Russell's situation. Sounds like the humans involved in his early life didn't help him adjust very well. When dogs do unacceptable behaviors from a human point of view, it is not the fault or responsibility of the dog. It is because the dog is INSUFFICIENTLY TRAINED, INSUFFICIENTLY SUPERVISED, and/or INSUFFICIENTLY SOCIALIZED or has a health-related issue.

What Russell is doing here is what he learned from his first human parents. Russell was taught and encouraged that it was ok to bark and challenge others (even his own kind) as a job he had in guarding his dog parent's personal property. Russell is now conditioned out of habit to doing these behaviors. Humans created this. The result: Russell is who he is at present.

I believe that anything that is learned can be unlearned and re-taught. For Russell, patience and his new environment are much needed. First, learning good obedience skills without confrontation or intimidation, along with lots of enthusiasm and rewards for compliance, will start to create new and more pleasant memories for Russell, making the old habits and memories less important. This takes patience and consistency. It is important for his new human leaders to understand that dogs only live in the moment and that they base their next decision on how to live and act in the next moment on things they have experienced (good, bad and otherwise) in the past. Creating new and more exciting experiences with patience and small successful steps will help the process be successful.

Good obedience and gradual exposure to humans under new and pleasant circumstances will help Russell learn to "trust" these new experiences (as trust is what is needed here) and give him a sound and stable quality of life. This will not happen over night and should be done under the guidance of a patient trainer that can understand and empathize with his past so that his future can be more fulfilling and complete.

Yours,
Uncle Duffy

April 12

| **TO:** | **Uncle Duffy** |
| **FROM:** | **Dusty** |

Ok. I understand. What you're saying, Uncle Duffy, is that Russell needs an Uncle Duffy like you. You need to understand that I'm not giving you up, but I will share you. Russell and other dogs like him need to have parents who are willing to learn to speak and understand "dog" so that they can learn to trust humans again.

Dusty

Dusty's friend Penny

April 13

TO: **Uncle Duffy**
FROM: **Dusty**
SUBJECT: **My new buddy nips people when she gets excited!**

Dear Uncle Duffy,

Dusty here. My newest friend is a St. Bernard. She's four months old and has lots of fun nipping at people when she is excited—sort of like I used to do with my litter mates and my mom. I get a kick out of watching her do it, but humans don't like it. Does she need some behavior modification?

Dusty

April 14

TO: **Dusty**
FROM: **Uncle Duffy**
SUBJECT: **Play biting**

Dear Dusty,

Your new friend is like you were when you were a puppy. Play biting is a way of having fun and at the same time testing your environment. We have to remind humans that in your world, Dusty, the dog that bites everyone else the most is the most dominant and the dog that gets bitten the most is the most subordinate. In between are all the other levels of the pecking order, much like the steps of a ladder. These levels are also in a constant state of shifting and adjusting as dogs mature and learn new things. Remember, in a dog's view of the world, if they can jump on it, bite it, or pee on it, they rule it. ☺

Play biting and jumping are dominance type behaviors that are not necessarily harmful behavioral issues. It is natural for dogs to test their environments and pack members (human or canine) and, by the feedback they receive, understand what their roles and statuses are in a particular social order. Human children do the same thing in different ways, such as crying to be picked up, or even screaming and throwing tantrums. These things being normal (in testing new surroundings, pack members, and circumstances) doesn't mean if let go or not redirected, they can't become behavioral problems!

We as humans sometimes inadvertently give permission (in play biting, for example) to dogs when they are very young (say, six to eight weeks old), by letting them chew on and bite our fingers because we think it is cute and young puppies are so cuddly. This first "imprinting" starts formulating future habits that the dogs think are ok. After all, from when they first remember us, we let them. Then when they get a bit older (like your new friend here), it is no longer cute and those sharp teeth really hurt human skin. Now we react differently by getting angry, yelling "No" at the dogs and/or holding their mouths shut.

The yelling at a puppy can create apprehension and anxiety, and a tradeoff behavior, such as submissive wetting and cowering, can occur. One of the most productive ways of helping a dog learn that play biting humans is not acceptable is what I refer to as the "timeout. This I did to you, Dusty, when we first met. As a dog species, you and your friends are one of the top five social creatures on the planet. So, when you as dogs break the social rules in your dog pack, you are shunned by the pack for a time. In your language, this means, "If you cannot behave around us, you cannot be around us for a time." This process you instinctively understand. As humans, we can invoke this discipline when teaching you that play biting us is not acceptable. This is done by putting you in your crate or another room for a short time.

Crates are not for punishment but can help with discipline!

It has always been suggested that the crate not be used for punishment. First of all, it is not necessary to "punish" a dog (an already submissive species), but "discipline" is necessary in any social order. Not using the crate as "punishment" was suggested because the traditional method of letting a dog know that you as their human leader are unhappy with something is to say "No" in a stern and authoritative voice. If this was done while putting a dog in a crate or another room, the dog (who does not understand what "No" means) would forget what he had just done and try concentrating on what this angry "No" tone is all about. He would then get frustrated in the crate or other room. To compound the problem, most humans think that because they stopped the behavior at that moment, the situation is solved. It is not! It is important when letting the dog back out of the crate or other area that you then show the dog what behavior IS acceptable and reward him for compliance. This, however, is not done, so the revolving-door-process of yelling "No" continues without solution.

Timeouts!

"Timeout" (like I did with you, Dusty), is a non-confrontational process that helps dogs realize what is unacceptable and provides an alternative, fun behavior instead. You see, play biting is a "demand" for attention. An unacceptable one. So, human leaders need to learn to take away what the dog is demanding. Attention from the human leader! This is done by instantly taking the dog (after he play bites) by his collar and walking him to his crate or to another enclosed room where you can shut a door, and putting him in it and then walking away. The key to it working is to SAY NOTHING TO THE DOG! Not "No", not "You're naughty", NOTHING!

This "freezes the moment". Remember dogs only live in the moment so controlling that helps you maintain attention. Maintaining attention allows learning to take place. (If you say anything, you change and create a new moment and the dog now concentrates on that). So, you want the dog to remember that his last act, play biting you, the human leader, socially deprived him of what he wanted most. You! This is one of the best disciplines to use and what is more important, the dog can relate to and understand what it means. Human leaders may have to repeat this a few times, depending on how stubborn their dogs are, but it will work if done consistently. Remember, dogs learn by mimic, repetition, and observation. The real neat thing is that there is no yelling or getting stressed, just depriving the dog of what he is demanding. Then, once you let the dog back out of the crate or other room, you show the dog what it is he CAN do to get the attention from you that he wants. Something such as a simple obedience skill like a "sit", for which you praise and reward him works very well. Before long, the dog will adjust his own behavior out of respect, not from fear and confrontation from the human leader.

Pass this on, Dusty, as this will help.

Yours,
Uncle Duffy

April 15

TO:	**Uncle Duffy**
FROM:	**Dusty**
SUBJECT:	**Play biting and timeouts!**

Dear Uncle Duffy,

I do remember timeouts. I still get them sometimes, because "play biting" is still FUN!!

Dusty

April 16

TO:	**Uncle Duffy**
FROM:	**Dusty**
SUBJECT:	**The "nervous Nellie" dog**

Dear Uncle Duffy,

One of my friends is a two-year-old female Shepherd/Lab mix. She claims to have been "rescued", but I don't know from what. She's always been timid and nervous and just ignored me and other dogs when we saw each other walking, except for a "hello sniff". Lately, though, she's been barking and lunging at us. She is starting to challenge us more and her parents are really embarrassed by it and now take her on walks at night when the rest of us are inside. I really miss her. Sounds like a behavior problem to me, Uncle Duffy. What do you think?

Dusty

April 17

TO: **Dusty**
FROM: **Uncle Duffy**
SUBJECT: **Re the "nervous Nellie" dog**

Dear Dusty,

It sounds like your friend is no longer timid and is beginning to assert herself and becoming more territorial when on leash with her humans to cover up her insecurity. Being a bit timid, she has learned over time that when she has become uncomfortable when new dogs and people come around, if she barks and carries on, they go away. She doesn't realize that they were going to keep walking anyway and so she thinks her barking has made it happen. She continues to think this way because her new human leaders are not redirecting her to a more acceptable activity. This same type of thing happens with dogs who bark at people they see out of their windows at home when those same people are walking down the street. They think that their barking makes the people go away, so they win this imaginary confrontation, resulting in the escalating and continuance of the activity.

Some fun obedience training would be in order here to help first in building up your friend's confidence and the feeling of having a job and purpose. Secondly, it would allow for better socialization training from her human leaders, as they would then have a means to redirect her to something she knows and likes doing when new people and situations are encountered. This would help her realize in a fun and non-confrontational way that people and dogs walking by are natural, everyday events. Nothing to get excited or stressed about. Odds are, if every time new people and dogs walked in her area, she was directed by human leaders to sit and have manners with enthusiastic praise and even treats for compliance, she would learn to look forward to seeing and meeting new people, much like you do today, Dusty. If you remember, you didn't handle new encounters very well at first either. ☺

First, however, it is important that she and her human leaders learn good obedience skills so that they can be properly applied in different situations and circumstances. This helps a lot when dogs are learning how to act in new social situations. Human leaders should always remember that dogs learn situationally, so there is generally a bit of stress and apprehension at first, especially with shy or introverted dogs. It is at these times that dogs can be made more comfortable if they have something they like doing with and for their human leader to fall back on. A large part of dog handling and leadership by humans is to make sure they never put their dogs in a situation they cannot (by lack of training) handle or are too immature to handle. Human Leadership skills, when working with dogs, are designed to anticipate and prevent unacceptable behaviors in the dogs by knowing the dogs' skills and limitations at any given moment, so as to never ask the dogs to do something they can't yet do. These things are needed here to help your friend get better social skills and more confidence.

Yours,
Uncle Duffy

April 17

| **TO:** | **Uncle Duffy** |
| **FROM:** | **Dusty** |

This makes sense. I remember when my social skills weren't too good. You remember—the first sleepover when Nitro rolled me? I sure learned my lesson.

Dusty

Dusty's friend Heady

Dusty's friend Jazzy

April 18

TO:	**Uncle Duffy**
FROM:	**Dusty**
SUBJECT:	**WOW! What an attitude!**

Dear Uncle Duffy,

A new dog I just met is a three-year-old Newfy/Lab mix. He told me that when he was four months old, he was adopted from a shelter. Before that he had been abused, and he was a very angry puppy. His new family spent a lot of time training and loving him and he turned out to be a very good, smart, loving dog (sounds a little like me, doesn't he?). He never leaves the yard. He brings his bowl to his family when he needs water. He carries the plastic grocery bags with his food inside into the house. He pulls kids on a sled in the wintertime and plays in the sandbox with them. He does lots of cool things. But oops! He has suddenly copped an attitude. He growls at his family when they tell him to do something he doesn't want to do. Personally, I say, "You go, dog," because he gets out of doing things when he does this. I'd like to try it, but something tells me you will disagree. What do you think, Uncle Duffy?

Dusty

April 19

TO:	**Dusty**
FROM:	**Uncle Duffy**
SUBJECT:	**Wow! What an Attitude!**

Dear Dusty,

Actually, Dusty, it may be possible that your friend might not be feeling very well. As you wrote, he does a lot of fun, cool things that he really seems to enjoy. It also sounds like he has a fun, loving, and caring new human family.

Now if his family has suddenly changed the way they ask him to do something and are not being respectful and nice as they used to be, that might explain his attitude. But there are a lot of things here that you and I don't necessarily know regarding what has taken place recently.

First, a good rule of thumb to go by when humans encounter something like this with their dogs (a sudden and radical change of interactive behavior) is to check for a health problem. Dogs can endure a great deal of discomfort without showing it, as in their pack, to show this may indicate weakness and thus a loss of status that is so important in a dog's view of the world.

Statistics indicated in a recent study of 1000 dogs that demonstrated sudden behavioral pattern changes that 20% had health-related issues. It is always good to deal with the health issue before attempting to deal with changing the behavior.

Another thing to remember here is that our dogs live in the moment. They make decisions on how to live in the next moment based on situations and things they have encountered and learned in the past. These things are called "triggers". Humans have certain triggers (good and bad) that they have from past experiences. These "triggers" (or, good or bad memories) sometimes set off angry as well as joyous responses to new situations we encounter that we find similar. This is also found to be the case in dogs. As your friend has a past history of certain abuses, it is possible that one of his new family members may have inadvertently responded to him in a way that set off one of his negative memories or "triggers", and this would explain his attitude due to the stress of this memory.

It is important to understand as much as possible about his past so that these negative "triggers" (that were created by other humans who were not as loving and respectful of him as his new family is) are not accidentally activated.

His new human leaders should take a look at these two possibilities (the health issue and the possible "triggers") and try to better evaluate where the problem is. Once this is known, it will be easier to correct.

Yours,
Uncle Duffy

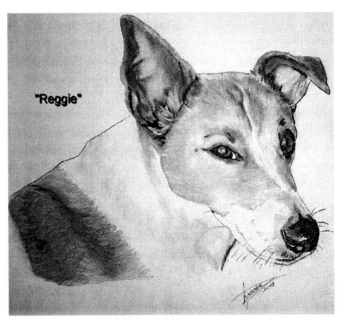

Dusty's friend Reggie

Dusty's friend Oreo

Dusty's friend Samantha

"DEXTER"

Dusty's friend Dexter

April 20

TO: **Uncle Duffy**
FROM: **Dusty**
SUBJECT: **A new roommate is coming! What to do?**

Dear Uncle Duffy,

Dusty here. Trouble is approaching. I'm sure of it. My next-door neighbor is a four-year-old male Cocker Spaniel. He lives with his human mom and dad and sister, who is going to college soon. Would you believe she (the soon-to-be college student) brought a male Jack Russell Terrier puppy home? The Cocker Spaniel is very jealous and possessive when another male dog is around (believe me, I know this firsthand). These two guys will have to live together for awhile. Do you think they will get along? I'm not very optimistic—just my opinion.

Dusty

April 21

TO: Dusty
FROM: Uncle Duffy
SUBJECT: There can be only one leader of the pack!

Dear Dusty,

As you know, in a dog pack there can be only one leader, particularly when the pack members are of the same gender. These two will be able to get along, providing the human leaders understand dog pack hierarchy rules.

You see, the Cocker Spaniel was there first. So all this time he has understood where his place is with his family. In a dog pack there can be only one leader of the pack.

Here is how the human leaders can make sure that this goes smoothly.

They can reduce the chances that these two will fight if they understand that there is no equality in a dog's social structure. Only one of these dogs can be top dog. This will only change if the dominant dog becomes injured, sick, or is no longer willing to demonstrate and proclaim his dominant position and status. Right now it appears that the first dog (the Cocker Spaniel) is in the dominant position. The human leaders can help keep this process under control in several ways.

First, they must not try to treat the dogs as equals. By trying to treat the dogs equally, it will only stress and anger the dominant dog and force him to declare and assert himself in ever more forceful ways, even by attacking the second dog. What must be done here is to edify the first dog by petting him first, greeting him first, letting him enter and exit doorways first, feeding and playing with him first, etc. This should only be changed by the human leaders if it is becoming clear that the two have switched positions. It does not sound like that in this case.

If the human leaders edify and honor the status of the dominant dog, he will not need to edify and assert himself. The result is, the pack hierarchy will stabilize.

Here are some things that the human leaders can look for to determine which dog is the dominant dog.

First, the dominant dog will push and crowd in front of the subordinate dog at doorways and when greeting the human leader. (He is saying that he is to be first, as it is his privilege for being leader).

Secondly, the dominant dog will climb on and mount the back of the subordinate dog to show dominance.

Third, the dominant dog will guard and keep toys to himself and even attempt to prevent the subordinate dog from eating its food. (The social rules in a dog pack are that dog pack leaders get the choice sleeping spots, are first to eat, first to drink, and first to play with and keep special toys).

And lastly, the dominant dog will go to the area where the subordinate dog is resting and force him to give that area up so the dominant dog can have it.

Subordinate dogs do not do these things back. So, if the human leaders watch for these signs, they will be able to determine which dog is dominant and edify him properly. This in turn will keep the peace.

Yours,
Uncle Duffy

April 22

TO:	**Uncle Duffy**
FROM:	**Dusty**
SUBJECT:	**I need a job—me, Dusty!**

Dear Uncle Duffy,

Dusty here. I think I need a job—you know, so I can help my mom with our living expenses. I want a cool job. Something like finding drugs for policemen, working for the FDA sniffing out food in people's suitcases, or, and this is the best idea, being a protector! Will you help me get a job?

Dusty

P.S. Don't let my mom get me a job as a model. She thinks I am the cutest dog in the whole wide world and would like to see me in that TV box. Yuk!

81

April 23

TO:	**Dusty**
FROM:	**Uncle Duffy**
SUBJECT:	**A special job for you, Dusty!**

Dear Dusty,

I think it is wonderful that you would like a special job! You, like all dogs, love learning new things and it helps give a sound sense of purpose. All living things need this. That is why I believe training is ongoing for the life of a dog. There is not one particular time that is best to start training, as you learned, Dusty. Remember, your training began as a very young puppy!

As far as sniffing out food in people's suitcases, I think the FDA probably has a lot of help in that area already, but there are other things you (and other dogs with certain special traits) can learn to do. Dogs of all breeds, shapes and sizes are being trained to help humans in areas of narcotics detection, search and rescue, explosives detection, article search, crowd control, therapy for the sick and handicapped, and there are now even dogs that can sniff out certain cancers.

With a nose estimated to be one million times more sensitive than that of a human, your species has much to offer humans in saving lives and understanding more about our environment.

Dusty, you already are a protector of your human mom by bonding with her as a part of your pack. There are special training procedures that teach dogs protection training that are used in law enforcement and the military. These dogs need constant practice and weekly training sessions to help maintain their skills. For the average human dog leader, this training would not be practical due to the necessity of the continued practice and training necessary as well as the risks of injury.

You are already helping your human mom with a job. You are writing this book to help humans better understand their dog pack members. By helping humans look at things from a dog's point of view, you will be better able to close the communication gap between us, as we have much to learn from each other.

You keep doing what you are doing and we will ask your human mom to look into some of these other training programs to see where you might be the most successful.

Yours,
Uncle Duffy

April 24

TO:	**Uncle Duffy**
FROM:	**Dusty**
SUBJECT:	**My cousin is afraid of storms!**

Dear Uncle Duffy,

My cousin is a scaredy cat (dog, really). She gets very upset before, during, and after thunderstorms. They don't bother me a bit. Well, a couple of times I've jumped up and barked when one of those loud claps of thunder startled me, but most of the time they don't bother me much. When I'm in my crate, I don't even notice a storm is happening. But my cousin...she just gets hysterical. Behavior problem again?

Dusty

Dusty's friends Jake and Mattie

Dusty's friend Sparky

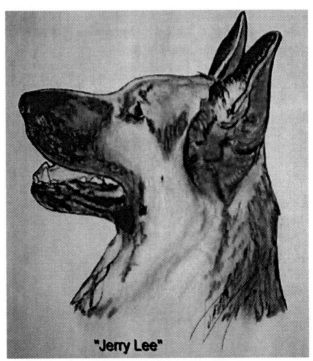

Dusty's friend Jerry Lee

Dusty's friends Jarrett, Gordon, and Georgette

Dusty's friend Sullivan

April 25

TO:	**Dusty**
FROM:	**Uncle Duffy**
SUBJECT:	**Your cousin has Thunderstorm Anxiety!**

Dear Dusty,

I feel bad for your cousin. This fear you are describing is called "thunderstorm anxiety". This occurs with dogs that have a natural sensitivity to barometric pressure changes that occur with sudden changes in weather conditions. For example, part of the sensitivity can be in the ears. It is estimated that a dog can hear things at 150-200 ft away that a human hears clearly at 20 ft away.

So one can imagine how a series of loud claps of thunder would impact a sensitive dog. Humans can also inadvertently contribute to the problem and make it worse by giving excessive attention and coddling when their dog gets stressed.

If the dog has a severe problem where she becomes uncontrollable in her fear, it is recommended that a program (set up by an experienced trainer in this area) be done to help recondition the dog to the noise of the thunderstorm. To simplify the explanation of the process, there is a series of thunderstorm sounds on tape that are played for the dog over a sometimes lengthy time period, gradually increasing the volume as the dog becomes conditioned to the noise and the stress lessens. This can be done in combination with certain medications (prescribed by a vet) to help the dog relax, along with giving the dog certain things to do, such as specific interactive obedience skills with her human leader, which helps take her mind off her anxiety. This is a specific behavior modification process.

This re-conditioning shows the dog alternatives to her fears and helps her realize that mother nature's flair-ups are normal events and nothing to be so upset about.

Sometimes with milder cases, something as simple as cotton balls in the dog's ears to help muffle the sounds (providing the dog will leave them in) in conjunction with a fun activity with her human leader, helps reduce the stress. Just don't forget to take the cotton balls out once the storm passes.

Some dogs relieve their own stress by going under a bed, into their kennel crate, or some other place they find secure to lay quietly. When they do this, the human leaders should not make over them and leave them be. The dog is dealing with it and to make over them unnecessarily can actually create a problem or make it worse.

Thunderstorms and bad weather are not pleasant, so it should be remembered that a dog's senses are more acute than a human's in certain areas and can result in the dog being a bit more sensitive.

Understanding and being proactive are needed from the human leader, not enablement.

Yours,
Uncle Duffy

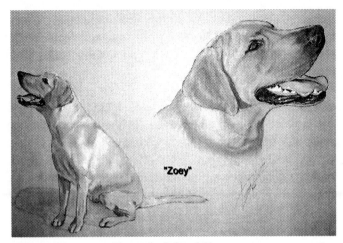

Dusty's friend Zoey

Dusty's friends Miss Wonderful, Whimsey, and Willie

April 26

TO:	Uncle Duffy
FROM:	Dusty
SUBJECT:	Chicken bones—how can I get some?

Dear Uncle Duffy,

Dusty here. I and my friends love knuckle bones and we love chicken. Why can't we have chicken bones? My mom shrieks if I ever find one that someone has thrown on the ground. It smells so yummy, but she really gets upset if I chew it up. What's the problem? Does my mom just hate chickens?

Dusty

April 27

TO:	Dusty
FROM:	Uncle Duffy
SUBJECT:	Chicken bones

Dear Dusty,

It is totally natural for dogs to like bones, and I know that you are no exception, ☺ and no, your mom doesn't hate chickens!

However, it has been found that chicken bones (being small) have a tendency to splinter, as dogs don't always chew thoroughly like humans do and these sharp splinters can seriously injure the stomach and digestive track of the dog. This can lead to serious complications, even death.

So, Dusty, as your human mom is responsible for your care, safety, and well being, as well as loving you very much, she will not give you chicken bones because they can be more harmful than any benefit you would get from them.

Beef knuckle bones, however, are safe and can be found in pet stores. They do not splinter and dogs can spend hours chewing on and enjoying them. Some dogs with sensitive stomachs or that are on special diets should not have these, as they may be a bit rich for their systems. If human leaders have any reservations about these bones or even rawhide chews, they should consult with their vets about their specific dogs and follow that advice.

Yours,
Uncle Duffy

April 27

| TO: | **Uncle Duffy** |
| FROM: | **Dusty** |

I understand what you are saying, but if I find 'em first, you know I'm gonna eat 'em.

Dusty

April 28

TO:	**Uncle Duffy**
FROM:	**Dusty**
SUBJECT:	**My friend goes nuts at some kinds of noises!**

Dear Uncle Duffy,

I have an Australian Cattle Dog friend. He actually is a Red Heeler. He's 4 years old, neutered (so am I), healthy, and very active. He is VERY ANXIOUS, though. Here's what he does: he bites when he is afraid or anxious. Noises seem to trigger his anxiety. These kinds of noises: telephone rings, motorcycles speeding by, sudden outside noises, a knock at the door. He goes into a massive panting and "fight" (not flight) mode whenever he hears something. He runs around the yard and barks aggressively. He hates roller bladers, bicycles, motorized scooters, and kids. They really "set him off". He does go to a dog run located right across the street from my house. When he's there, he doesn't show any aggression towards people. He tends to herd and referee us other dogs while he's there. He is obsessive compulsive about his tennis ball and plays catch. I just think he's always operating in "panic mode" and I'm concerned about him. He is very wary of strangers and will be defensive with new people so I don't know if you will be able to work with him. What do you think, Uncle Duffy?

Dusty

April 29

TO:	**Dusty**
FROM:	**Uncle Duffy**
SUBJECT:	**Noises**

Dear Dusty,

It sounds like there may be a multitude of issues that are affecting your friend's behavior, but first, it is best to check for any health-related issues that could be affecting him and making him more sensitive. Sudden noises and sounds may indicate a hearing disorder that frightens and stresses him, so lashing out by biting or nipping would be a natural response. It just isn't a safe one. Checking for a hearing disorder may be appropriate.

If a hearing and health problem are ruled out, then it is likely that these noises, associated with specific behaviors from humans, have been negative "triggers" for him in the past and have caused him trauma. (I talked about "triggers" earlier in this book.) The noises you describe are all ones that have specific pitches of sound that seem to set him off. Skate boarding, bicycles, motor cycles, etc., are not around him when he is in the dog run so the trigger seems to be these activities and/or sounds. The fast movements of these activities are also something that could stress him, as he can't herd them (which is his nature), because of their speed. His obsession for herding and gathering is not fulfilled with these activities, so exposure to them without an alternative job or fun function for him to do results in building up his stress.

His human leaders should take him to a vet for a health check and then try to create an environmental and training scenario that doesn't put your friend in a situation that he is too unprepared or too immature to handle based on his genetic makeup.

When evaluating behavior, there is a little mathematical formula that helps put it into perspective. It is: GENETICS + ENVIRONMENT = BEHAVIOR.

Genetics is defined as what the dog is born with; what is already there. It cannot be altered. It is who and what the dog is about. Environment in this case is defined as where the dog lives; under what conditions; what he learns by accident, on purpose, or by omission of responsibility; and what other social exposure has taken place, positive or negative. These two things, genetics and environment combined, result in the behavior displayed.

So, if there is an aspect of our dog's behavior that as human leaders we find unacceptable, we cannot go into the genetics and fix it. It is too late. We need to go into the environment and find the "triggers" that set the behaviors off. Remove, alter, redirect, or adjust them, and the behavior will change. It may not

occur all at once. It has taken your friend (who is 4 years old) four years to get this way. But it *can* change with patience, understanding, and consistency. It is said that anything that is learned can be un-learned and re-taught. I agree wholeheartedly with this. Old dogs can learn new tricks, so to speak.

Yours,
Uncle Duffy

May 1

| **TO:** | **Uncle Duffy** |
| **FROM:** | **Dusty** |

I'm looking forward to getting old so I can learn new tricks!

Dusty

Dusty's friend Shadow

Dusty's friend Lala

May 2

TO: **Uncle Duffy**
FROM: **Dusty**
SUBJECT: **This dog is very destructive when his family is not home.**

Dear Uncle Duffy,

I recently met a dog who destroys pillows, furniture, and other things in his house when his family is away. I would never do that, Uncle Duffy. Is something wrong with him?

Dusty

May 3

TO: **Dusty**
FROM: **Uncle Duffy**
SUBJECT: **Your friend may suffer from Separation Anxiety.**

Dear Dusty,

There are a number of different reasons why this destructiveness can occur, depending on whether this is a puppy or an older dog. With a puppy, it may have to do with a teething issue along with boredom. With an older dog, it is usually out of boredom, frustration of being alone, something going on outside that is out of the ordinary and can't be smelled or identified, or even separation anxiety (which is the fear of being left alone away from pack members--a high degree of stress when isolated).

These "triggers" can manifest themselves in compulsive types of behaviors, such as destructiveness, digging, even something as extreme as chewing on themselves.

If this is not overly severe, where the dog is injuring itself, the amount of frustration felt by the dog can be reduced and the destructive behavior corrected by shrinking down the area in which the dog stays. This is where crate training is very valuable. Dusty, the behavior you are describing indicates that the dog is faced with a situation that he is unprepared or too immature to handle. So, the human leaders need to restrict the space the dog is in to something it *can* handle and at the same time give the dog something productive and fun to do.

This doesn't mean that the dog should be in a crate 8-12 hours per day. That is excessive. Three-five hours per day for an adult dog is not unreasonable. But the crate is a place where the dog should be if it cannot be monitored for its own safety and protection. It is the dog's parents' right as leaders to control space. A mother dog with her litter will confine the puppies to a particular area where she can better monitor them for their safety. We as human leaders should do no less.

A crate, a fenced yard, an outside kennel run are all space leadership tools that help protect dogs from the dangers of our environment and even from themselves. Dusty, tell your friend's human parents to put the dog in a crate when they are going to be gone for awhile, turn the radio on with soft music, and give the dog a favorite chew bone or special crate toy like that hollow rubber toy you have (available at your local pet store) with a gob of peanut butter or crèam cheese on the inside of it. (You know how to describe this, Dusty. You love this part of staying alone.) Your friend will spend hours trying to get the peanut butter or cream cheese out of the toy, and, at the same time, his stress will be reduced. Remind the human leaders that it is very important to remember that when they let the dog out of the crate, they pick up and put away the crate toy until next time. This way the dog will not be bored with it left in the crate and will think it is brand new each time. This enables the human leaders to show control of objects. This is an alpha leader's right (to control objects) and is respected. Besides, the dog will look forward to getting it again from them as a reward for going back in the crate at their next request, making this a fun event. (It works for you, doesn't it, Dusty?)

In getting dogs used to crates, human leaders should start putting the dog in it with a special treat or toy 2-3 times per day for 10 to 30 minutes each time while they are at home engaged in normal routines. This sets up the learned conditioning process that being ignored part of the time is not a terrible thing, but a normal everyday event that is also fun. You see, a dog that learns to be ignored part of the time while people are at home is less likely to develop separation anxiety when people leave home. I even suggest feeding the dog in the crate so that eating is a private time that does not have to be disturbed and is a special event.

Dogs are naturally den animals so a crate (a dog's household den), can and will be a place of sanctuary, security, and privacy that the dog loves, respects, and looks forward to.

For the price of a kennel crate and a $6 toy, human leaders can save thousands of dollars in destroyed household furnishings, vet bills for removal of harmful objects that have been swallowed, and unnecessary anger and frustration with their dogs.

Dogs do not naturally know what is expected of them when living in our environment. It is our responsibility to show them in a way that they can relate to and have fun with. Right, Dusty?

Yours,
Uncle Duffy

May 4

TO:	**Uncle Duffy**
FROM:	**Dusty**

Boy, do I understand that! I was so scared when I first came to my new mom's home because I didn't know how to deal with my new surroundings until I was taught step by step. Now I have a GREAT life!!

Dusty

May 5

TO:	**Uncle Duffy**
FROM:	**Dusty**
SUBJECT:	**Car Chasing**

Dear Uncle Duffy,

Two of my neighbors, Oscar and Max, love to chase cars. They are always on leash, but they take off after cars. (I do this every now and then myself.) Our parents get very frustrated with this. Are we being naughty bad?

Dusty

May 6

TO: **Dusty**
FROM: **Uncle Duffy**
SUBJECT: **Car Chasing**

Dear Dusty,

No, you are not being "naughty bad" from a dog's point of view because, as dogs, you love to chase things and love to be chased. This is genetically normal for a predator. However, it is unacceptable to do this activity when living with humans, as the cars you love to chase can hurt and/or kill you. So, to protect you dogs from yourselves, it is important that human leaders learn good obedience skills that provide a fun and safe alternative to this natural instinct to chase things.

An obedience technique such as the heel technique (walking properly, with manners, on a leash) is an excellent tool to redirect a dog from a natural behavior that may be harmful. to one more acceptable. Not only does the process of this technique need to be learned, but it also needs to be practiced under varying conditions, circumstances, and environments so that the dog knows what is expected as things change around him.

The human leader needs to be patient here to allow the dog to learn and adjust by being consistent, enthusiastic, and ready with praise and rewards for compliance. A dog walking properly on leash is very important in establishing proper communication between the dog and its human leader. You see, in a dog's view of the world, if he is out in front of his pack member or members (including the human leader), he thinks he is in charge and usually is. It is like us as humans being promoted to CEO of a major corporation. It is a big deal and can falsely give the dog permission to test human leadership in other areas. So the dog needs to learn that the human leader, as alpha leader, is in charge of the walk. Particularly when cars go by. ☺

By the same token, the leash and collar should never be used to yank on or punish the dog for non-compliance. Remember, in all learning, mistakes are made and that is all they are--mistakes. The leash is only there to help control space so that the human leader can show the dog what is expected in an area that can be properly controlled by the human leader. Learning should be fun. When it is, the learning comes faster and is retained longer.

Learning by fear and intimidation is only the learning and reinforcing of fear and intimidation, which is ultimately resented.

So when learning good obedience techniques, it is important for human leaders to seek out those trainers and processes that use leashes and collars as space control tools, not training tools. Human leaders are always responsible for teaching their dogs whatever they want them to learn. A leash and collar are not!

Yours,
Uncle Duffy

May 7

TO:	**Uncle Duffy**
FROM:	**Dusty**
SUBJECT:	**Too much barking!**

Dear Uncle Duffy,

Sometimes I just bark at everything when I'm outside. There are a lot of critters in my backyard. But I don't bark as much as my neighbor. She just won't shut up. Her parents got a ticket from the police. (My mom probably would have too except she makes me come in.) How can we keep ourselves from barking so much?

Dusty

May 8

TO:	**Dusty**
FROM:	**Uncle Duffy**
SUBJECT:	**Too much barking!**

Dear Dusty,

It is not about you keeping yourself from barking so much, but, rather, it is about the responsibility of the human leader to first find out why you are barking (as dogs bark for a reason), and then take the appropriate steps to redirect the behavior to a more desirable one.

Simply punishing a dog for its barking without figuring out why it is occurring and taking the steps to correct the cause is like a revolving door. The dog continues to bark and the human leader continues to be frustrated.

There are many reasons why a dog will bark--from boredom, to perceived intruders, to separation anxiety. Each case should be dealt with on an individual basis. But in most cases when a dog is barking at sounds, people, or animals it sees from inside a yard or house, it is announcing itself and claiming a territory, advising all that will listen that it is theirs. Barking also accentuates posturing to let any potential challenger know that there is something there and to be reckoned with if necessary. From inside a house or yard, the dog perceives over time that when it barks, people and other animals keep moving away, and it thus concludes that its announcement of its presence was successful in scaring them off. So it perceives that this action is successful and will continue it unless the human leader intervenes. Sometimes, however, these perceived intruders do not always move away, like a squirrel playing around outside a fence. The dog will continue to bark until it does go away. As one can guess, this can go on for a while and become a social nuisance.

In a lot of these cases, this is territorial in nature and the problem is that the dog's territory is too big for him to manage. This can be very frustrating for him, particularly those dogs with strong prey drives. The human leader should evaluate the situation they are in and make adjustments in the environmental conditions that the dog is dealing with, so the dog can better handle it in a more socially acceptable way.

It should be remembered that the dog is doing something very natural for a dog. It is not a wrong or right issue unless both parties (you as human leader and the dog) have a mutual understanding of right or wrong. This is not the case. Dogs do not have moral rights or wrongs in their view of the world. It simply works or it does not, and it feels good or it does not. So, like it says in the Loving Contract with You, My Dog (described earlier), the human leader should not put a dog in a situation he is too immature or unable to handle.

Excessive barking in most cases is the result of the dog being put in a situation and environmental conditions that are too overwhelming for him to manage. Human leaders can change the conditions by putting in new or different fencing, providing a smaller kennel run area away from the view of perceived intruders (animals and humans), or bringing the dog inside to a specific area or kennel crate.

Sometimes the best way to have a dog not do an unacceptable behavior is to simply not expose the dog to the "trigger" that could allow him to make a "mistake". A "mistake" is all it is, given the dog's view of the world without his leader there to show and teach him alternatives.

Yours,
Uncle Duffy

"Jordie"
Brittany Spaniel

Dusty's friend Jordie

"A Frozen Moment"   "Jordie"

May 9

TO: **Uncle Duffy**
FROM: **Dusty**
SUBJECT: **My friend is depressed because her brother died.**

Dear Uncle Duffy,

I feel so sorry for my friend whose dog brother died. She won't come out of her house and play. She still eats, but that's about all. She is very depressed. What can we do to help her?

Dusty

P.S. I miss her dog brother too.

May 10

TO:	**Dusty**
FROM:	**Uncle Duffy**
SUBJECT:	**Depression due to death of a companion**

Dear Dusty,

This is very sad. Humans know the feelings of loss of a loved one and companion. It seems to leave a hole in our world for a while and can be very unsettling. Dogs are creatures of habit, and the loss of bonded friends and pack members can alter normal routines in a very startling way that affects some dogs quite severely.

I believe that in the cycle of life when these holes of loss occur with the departing of our loved ones, that, like all holes, they are made to be filled again. The former content of the hole can never be replaced, but new content can be just as wonderful and renewing. Sometimes a new friend brought into the situation can more often than not refill (not replace) the hole of loss.

For your friend, a new companion may help take her mind off this loss and help her refocus on being herself again. After all, she is a dog that likes to play, chase things, and enjoy special treats and just love life. Her situation has changed, not ended. This can help the human leaders as well, as I'm sure they too feel the loss of your friend's dog brother.

I believe that our capacity to feel loss and grief is in direct proportion to our capacity to love. So being able to share with a new energetic friend all that was learned from her former dog brother and focusing her love on that new friend can and will be good for her as well as her human leaders.

Holes are meant to be filled back up!

Yours,
Uncle Duffy

May 12

TO:	**Duffy**
FROM:	**Dusty**
SUBJECT:	**Children**

Dear Uncle Duffy,

Dusty here. Today one of my mom's friends came over and brought her children. Wow! I was so excited. I have missed playing with my litter mates and was ready to play with these children. They were a little bigger than I am, but that doesn't matter. The children were ready to play too. They came running toward me, waving their hands and making funny sounds. I jumped up on the first one that came close and caught his t-shirt with my teeth. Got him! I started pulling and growling and carrying on the way I always did with my dog brothers and sisters. Next thing I knew, mom had stuck me in my crate. She didn't say a word to me either, which means I wasn't behaving correctly. I don't get it. My mom does seem to have trouble with play. (Remember my previous e-mail.)

Ok. So I got to come back out. The children came running at me again. This time I danced around them and nipped at them in my teasing way. Whoosh—back into my crate! @!#! I'm spending all my time in my crate and missing this opportunity to play with the children and have FUN. What is the matter with my mom?

Ok. Out again. I just quietly walked up to one of the children. Ouch! She poked her finger in my eye. Grrr! I saw mom coming. This time I ran, but she caught me, took hold of my collar, and marched me right into my crate, saying no words. That little girl poked her finger in my eye! That wasn't fair. Well, I was sorta tired anyway so I laid down to take a nap. Would you believe that same child sat down right in front of my crate and stuck her fingers in my face? I licked them, but she said I tried to bite them. I didn't. The child's mother yelled at me, but my mom didn't. She told the child to just leave me alone for awhile. At least my mom understood the situation this time.

Out again. Why? Because one of the children came over and let me out. I didn't get my nap so I was pretty hyper—just trying to stay awake and be sociable. The children were eating something—little chocolate candies. They made me sit and then gave me a candy. This time my mom got upset with the children. Chocolate is not good for dogs, I guess. Even though she wasn't mad at me, she put me back in my crate. I think she should have put the children in my crate and let me stay out—to just play by myself, I guess.

I'm very sad now. I wanted to play with the children, but now I think I don't like children.

Dusty

Dusty plays with children!

May 13

TO:	**Dusty**
FROM:	**Uncle Duffy**
SUBJECT:	**Children**

My dear friend Dusty,

This is a common problem and frustration for dogs, human leaders and human children alike. Like anything new, humans, as well as dogs, don't always know or understand how to deal and interact with each other at first. So, it is important that understanding and learning apply to dogs and children alike.

In order for this to work effectively, it is important that the human leader understands that s(he) must: 1) be in charge of the interaction between dogs and children to make sure each can enjoy the other's company and 2) protect them from each other. ☺ It is very important here that the dog views the human leader as a fair, kind, and consistent leader of the pack. In other words, the dog must see the human leader as the alpha leader (the one in charge). This will be particularly important when times arise where the human leader has to discipline a child or other dog pack member, if applicable. This way, the dog will not interfere and cause disruption.

The human leader should always be aware that a dog's view of things and its perception of the world are not like a human's. But it IS child-like. A dog's conceptual abilities can range from a 2-5- year-old human child and, in some breeds, even higher, but these conceptual abilities are still based on a dog's view and perspective of the world. For example, human children and human adults do not move the same. Human adults are bigger and are more sure and confident in their movements, presenting a more specific "leadership" or "alpha" appearance to the dog. Children, particularly younger children under the age of 10, have jerkier movements, can be a bit clumsy (depending on development), and, when angry or excited, they tend to react in exaggerated movements and very often end up venting their frustration or overexcitement toward the dog. The dog is the family member that appears to be the weakest and is unable to talk or tattle, so to speak.

The dog, although viewed at times as the perfect scapegoat, does not interpret things the same way. The child's body postures and excitement are viewed by the dog as another sibling, another "puppy" in which to interact with. So, if the child's behavior and body language are viewed by the dog as disruptive, the dog will attempt to discipline the child like it would another dog or puppy. This results in a nipping or even a bite, depending on how serious the infraction was viewed. If the child's behavior and body language are viewed by the dog as play (particularly chase and tug of war games), the dog may initiate play biting in these games the same as it would with another dog. Unfortunately, dogs do not and cannot understand that human skin cannot tolerate play biting and nipping the way a dog's skin can.

It is also important to remember here that a dog over the age of 7 months knows exactly how hard it is biting, just like a human knows how hard to grip something so that it breaks or does not break. A nip is meant to be a nip just as a hard bite is meant to be a hard bite. Dog bites on humans more often than not occur from the family pet, not from the abused or viciously trained dogs that make for exciting media coverage. These things occur from a lack of understanding on how dogs perceive things (an understanding of which would greatly help the human leaders to be more proactive) and not teaching children proper, respectful ways to play with and interact with dogs.

Dusty, for your benefit and the benefit of the children that you and your species love to play with, here are some do's and don'ts about interactions between children and dogs that should be very helpful. These rules of conduct should be strictly followed for their safety and protection.

****

First, a child should be taught to always ask permission before petting a dog and never approach or call a loose, unattended dog.

Children should be taught ***not to*** ....

- ***Pet a dog around the face and head!*** Pet the dog from the neck to the tail, not from the tail to the neck. If the dog is wearing a collar, the child should pet the dog from the collar back.

- ***Play tug of war games!*** Tug of war games are play aggression games between dogs and can escalate aggression toward humans, depending on temperament. Misjudging distance when grabbing at a tug toy can also result in an accidental bite. Teach fetch games instead, always having a second toy of the same type to throw to help teach the dog to give the first item up in exchange for another.

- *Tease the dog!* This only results in the dog viewing this as disruptive pack behavior that needs discipline (a bite in their world) or, worse, it brings out fear & aggression that can later endanger the child. Besides, it is simply cruel.

- *Disturb the dog when it is sleeping!* "Let sleeping dogs lie" is a good rule. Sometimes, like humans, dogs can be startled when suddenly awakened and be a bit disoriented. The reaction: possibly an accidental bite that never should have happened and a traumatized child and dog.

- *Bother the dog when it is eating!* Feeding times are very personal and important to a dog, as it is one of its three motivations: food, petting, and nice soothing tones. It is respectful that once food has been given, the dog is allowed to eat in peace. Feeding a dog in a kennel crate or other private area can help the human leaders best monitor and maintain peace.

- *Disturb the dog when it is chewing on a bone or toy!* Even though some dogs do not mind sharing their toys with humans, not all dogs are alike. So, this rule should apply to all dogs. Bones, for example, are very important to dogs and are to be respected. It is important that children learn to respect these things the same as it is important to train the dog on how to properly interact. Like feeding times, giving a dog a chew bone or special toy in a kennel crate or private area can help prevent accidental biting.

- *Bother dog when it is in a kennel crate!* A kennel crate is a marvelous space leadership tool and place of sanctuary for the dog. When the dog is in the crate eating or resting, children should not sit on the crate, poke fingers or objects into the crate, or yell and scream when the dog is inside. This can be very stressful and unsettling for the dog, and instead of the crate being a place of sanctuary, it becomes a place of torment.

- *Run from or chase the dog!* Dogs love to chase things and to be chased. It is a natural instinctive process for a predator. Although

107

it can seem like a lot of fun, injuries occur with the dog getting too excited and attempting to jump on and nip at the child. This is normal dog play and not meant disrespectfully, but, for obvious reasons, it is not appropriate in play with young humans. As in the No Tug of War rule above, an alternative game is the fetch game, which accommodates the dog's love of chasing things and is safe for the child.

Children should be…..

Involved in the training of the dog and be given certain responsibilities (under supervision) that can promote respect, love, and bonding between the dog and the child. This should be done following supervised socialization and the establishment of rules of conduct for the children and the dog. This training includes instruction for the child on how to have the dog "sit". This helps the dog look at and respect the child's position in its perceived pack hierarchy. (Remember, dogs don't perceive that they are part of a human family as we do; they are perceiving that they are part of a pack, as they understand it. So, ultimately, it will be their understanding, belief, and view of the situation that will dictate their actions). From learning the "sit", the child can then be given the responsibility of having the dog "sit" and then giving the dog its food, special treats, or favorite toys. This, too, helps the dog look at children as alpha leaders, by the acceptance of food and special things from them. This process then helps in teaching the dog to relinquish objects they are not allowed or objects that are dangerous for them without being confrontational, intimidating, having an unwanted tug of war, or chasing them around and getting more frustrated, which can result in aggressive responses from the dog.

Finally, human leaders should remember the following proactive rules when they have a young child and dog in the house…….

- *First, __NEVER__ leave your child and dog alone unattended for any reason, until the child is over 12 years old.*

- *Second, always be prepared to give your dog some quiet time from the child, where the child cannot bother it. This is calming, necessary, and the dog will see and respect your leadership, as will the child.*

- *Last, it is important to remember that not all dog breeds are compatible with your individual lifestyle. It is important to do your homework on what breed traits can be most compatible and, if necessary, get some professional input from a qualified trainer. Older dogs from shelters may not be a good pet if they have not been socialized with young children in their early development. Also, as dogs get older, they have more set patterns and habits as well as physical disorders that develop, which don't allow them the patience or ability to adapt as well with young children. These things should be evaluated so that you can choose the dog that is right for you and to help make sure you are right for them.*

Dusty, this should help, because dogs and children interacting and playing together is a wonderful thing. It can and will work if human leaders consistently teach the interaction between you and the children. I will work with your mom on this. As for you, give it another chance!

Yours,
Duffy

Dusty's friend Lexie

Today

Dusty has grown to love, respect, and even obey his mom. He heels, sits, stays, and comes when she calls, "Dusty, here!". He is a favorite in his neighborhood and loves the attention he receives when he goes on his daily walks with his mom. He has many friends, both human and dog. Dusty has also grown to love Duffy (whom he still affectionately calls "Uncle Duffy") and is quite fond of Duffy's wife, Auntie Jane, also a trainer. Given his attachment to Uncle Duffy and Auntie Jane, Dusty doesn't want to stop sending his e-mails. So...being the dominant aggressive dog that he is (personalities don't change), Dusty will continue his own "advice column" with his friends. He, Uncle Duffy, and Auntie Jane (in their unique working relationship) will continue to assist Dusty's friends and their human leaders in future problems that are both common and uncommon in continuing dog/human interaction.

For now, though, there is one thing that must always be remembered. Training doesn't stop when the organized sessions are completed. Training is ongoing, particularly as the dog grows and develops mentally and physically. Training and learning are lifetime processes that get better the more they are applied. Dogs are not machines, but living things that learn to adapt and change to new situations that occur around them. Much like us as.... Humans!

"Dusty"
Welsh Terrier
1 yr old

About Kninepal Training and Behavior Specialists Profiles

Duffy and Jane Lueder have been training dogs for a combined 35 years... not for the show ring, but for everyday problems that occur with people in their own backyards. They look at this

as not helping people with dog problems, but, rather, "HELPING DOGS WITH PEOPLE PROBLEMS!"

Duffy started a successful law enforcement career in 1972 with the Washington, D.C., police department. He was recruited to the Georgetown University police department, the Falls Church, Virginia, police department, and finally retired from law enforcement in 1992 from the Wexford County sheriff department in northern Michigan.

In 1981 Duffy became a certified police K-9 handler and six months later became a certified handler/trainer and opened his new Dog Obedience Training Center.

With a total of over 2500 hours of additional instruction and education over the years, Duffy is a certified handler/trainer in obedience, man-tracking, narcotics detection, image training, building search, crowd control, and explosives detection. From 1985-1988 he was one of only seven explosives dog handlers in the state of Michigan.

In addition to K-9 handling, his public relations officer duties, and his dog training center, Duffy also became one of the first 62 D.A.R.E officers in Michigan. D.A.R.E. (Drug Abuse Resistance Education) is a program wherein police officers are specially trained to teach 5th and 6th graders a 17-week course on resisting the pressures to take drugs.

Duffy designed, taught, and implemented one of the first drug education programs for the workplace following the enactment of the Drug-Free Workplace Act in the state of Michigan. This included not only lectures and on-site employee drug education, but incorporated (with the support of management and employee representatives) the on-site private use of trained drug dogs in areas open to the public as well.

Since his retirement in 1992, Duffy has continued to train dogs for people of all walks of life, including the handicapped, as he himself had become handicapped at retirement. He further developed the KNINEPAL TRAINING & BEHAVIOR MODIFICATION PROGRAM for dogs and their owners as it is taught today. He is also an approved evaluator for the "CANINE GOOD CITIZEN" program (CGC). (Learn more about CGC at www.akc.org).

Jane, who has worked right alongside Duffy, also worked with children in foster care and assisted Duffy with drug education for children and adults alike. She was an active member of a service group known as the Sheriff's Posse, an organized search and rescue unit that used horses to assist in locating missing and lost persons and to conduct other civic safety functions. She also served as  the first female special deputy on the sheriff department and worked with Duffy as an emergency back-up K-9 handler.

Jane is an excellent rider and in her love for horses, has worked with everything from Belgium's to wild Mustangs. Her favorites, however, are Paints.

Jane became a certified obedience trainer in 1986 and has worked beside Duffy ever since, specializing in puppies and health aspects related to training. She also developed extensive experience with other animals as well when she managed and operated a pet shop for two years and dealt with everything from dogs and cats to birds and fish. She also became an experienced assistant vet tech and practice manager for a Georgia veterinarian.

As a working team, Duffy and Jane have assisted people from all walks of life with many different breeds of dogs with their individual behavioral problems and quirks. This has become their specialty, as they have expanded their education and experience into this area. As a result, they have one-on-one (not in groups), hands-on experience training with over 2000 individual families and over 4000 individual dogs over the years.

Duffy and Jane now live and work in the Georgia, South Carolina area, where they make "house calls" on a daily basis. They continue to work with individual families and their dogs nationwide, providing consultation and assistance over the internet. To learn more about them and their training philosophy, visit them at: www.kninepal.com.

Index

A

B

bones 89, 90, 107

G

H

I

J

L

M

N

nipping 27, 67, 91, 106
noises 30, 90, 91
non-confrontational ways 13
normal interaction and communication among dogs 27
nose 4, 23, 82

O

obedience 4, 65, 66, 69, 71, 86, 97, 98, 112, 113
one-on-one instruction vii
overreact 8, 13

P

pack vi, 8, 9, 10, 11, 12, 13, 14, 17, 18, 39, 45, 46, 61, 68, 75, 80, 81, 82, 97, 102, 105, 107, 108
pack members 8, 11, 67, 80, 82
patience and consistency 65
pawing 17, 27
perceptions 15
personalities v, vii, 1, 10, 14, 15, 57, 111
  assertive 15
  dominant 67, 80, 111
  subordinate 67, 81
play 2, 6, 8, 9, 24, 25, 27, 28, 30, 31, 32, 35, 50, 54, 57, 63, 67, 68, 69, 70, 80, 81, 90, 101, 102, 103, 104, 106, 108
play biting 27, 67, 68, 69, 70, 106
potty 22, 23, 24, 60
protector dogs 81, 82

Q

quiet time 11, 108

R

regulating diet 24
reinforce the positive 17, 61
repetitions 11
retrieve 27
rewards 8, 9, 13, 17, 65, 95, 97
rule by biting 12

S

safety 18, 89, 95, 106, 113

Printed in the United States
66882LVS00004B/133-150